ON THE ROAD

Traveling Europe in a Campervan

Stephanie Rickenbacher & Lui Eigenmann

ON THE ROAD
by Campervan

SCHIFFER
PUBLISHING

4880 Lower Valley Road • Atglen, PA 19310

TABLE OF CONTENTS

Above: Tulip field in Lisse, Netherlands
Below: Beach house boardwalk in Aveiro, Portugal

Above: A stormy sea on the Wild Atlantic Way in Ireland
Below: Sveti Naum Monastery on Lake Ohrid in North Macedonia

The source of the Sava River is one of many in Triglav National Park.

About us

WHY WE'RE EMBARKING ON A JOURNEY ACROSS THE WHOLE OF EUROPE

A hike through Tara National Park in Serbia, a drive through the semidesert of Bardenas Reales in Spain, or a fishing trip at the North Cape in Norway:

Europe has much more to offer than one might believe. A look at the map reveals that there are forty-seven countries that together make up our continent, and every single one of these countries is incredible. Every single one of these countries hides at least one natural wonder, and in each of these countries, interested people live, just like you and me.

Over the past 2.5 years, we've made it our goal to travel to each of these forty-seven countries with a camper. You might be wondering why we didn't fly. Quite simply, there's no better way to explore Europe than with a camper. When you travel by plane, you often arrive in a city, stay there for one or two days, and then leave. With the camper, you experience a country as a whole. You enter at one border, cross the country, and exit at another border. So you experience the nature, the roads, the villages, and the cities.

But we also travel with a camper because we always have our bed with us. During our journey, we didn't have to unpack our suitcase every evening, look for accommodation, or deal with public transportation. With the camper, we stopped where we liked, without adhering to departure times, without following a plan; we were free. We spent the night in the most-beautiful places and had lunch at the most-exciting places. Like in Ireland on the Wild Atlantic Way. From a pull-off, we had an incredible view of the ocean, but hunger struck. No problem. We opened the fridge, turned on the gas stove, and, ten minutes later, could enjoy our meal at one of the most beautiful places in Europe.

Above: Enjoying alone time for two at the Furka Pass in the Swiss Alps
Below: One of the most beautiful campgrounds in Europe—Camping Lazy in Slovakia

You must know, we are adventurers, nature enthusiasts. We prefer to be outdoors, in all kinds of weather. For more than sixteen years now, we've been going through life as a couple and as a team, trusting and understanding each other blindly. Otherwise, this crazy 42,874-mile (69,000-kilometer) journey through Europe probably wouldn't have been possible. We encountered not only national borders but also our personal limits. We had to solve more than just one problem and rely on ourselves. But we made it, and behind us lies an unforgettable journey across our continent, which we want to share with all of you through this book.

With this journey, we "forced" ourselves into countries that we had never considered as vacation destinations. This includes countries that are unfortunately not as easy to visit today as they were during our grand European journey. It's precisely these unknown countries that have become dear to us. Their names are Serbia, Romania, or Lithuania, for example. Countries we barely knew before the trip, let alone locate them on the map. That's exactly what we wanted to change with our tour. We wanted to experience and feel our own continent, which has so much to offer. What good is it if we know Bali or Australia? Here in Europe, we are at home, and right here, you can find (almost) everything you often seek far away.

There are hot springs in Spain, primeval forests in Poland, an ice cave in Romania, or dolphins in the Bosporus. Each of the forty-seven countries in Europe has its treasures, sometimes well hidden, sometimes already known. In this book, we reveal the highlights: where you can go horse fishing in Belgium, where the wild horses hide in Bosnia, or where you can find the most-beautiful views. We'll tell you about the most-scenic camping spots, the most-extraordinary restaurants, and which language to use to communicate best in Kosovo.

Our journey as presented in this book contains forty-two countries. In our trip, we visited forty-five, including Russia, Belarus, and Ukraine. We had a full visit in Ukraine, and we also set foot in Russia and took a bike tour through Belarus. However, out of an abundance of caution, we have not included our experiences in Russia and Belarus due to geopolitical developments. Similarly, travel to Ukraine is not recommended. We have presented our experiences in Ukraine simply as a reminiscence of our past experiences there, but not as a travel guide.

Come with us on a journey through the whole of Europe, a journey with thirty-seven tours through forty-two countries and cultures, and let yourself be inspired for your next camper trip. We'll also share a lot about ourselves, the breakdowns and problems we faced on the road, where we reached our limits, and why Iceland and Kazakhstan are still missing.

We like to sum up our 2.5-year adventure with the words "Europe is awesome."

Steffi Rickenbacher & Lui Eigenmann

Above: Sunset on the Côte d'Azur
Below: Looking at the Azure Window through our kitchen window on Gozo

Our *Campervan: Purchase* and *Modification* Tips

WHAT WE REALLY NEED ON THE ROAD

A campervan is very personal and, especially with custom builds, as individual as its owner. Thanks to the numerous rental campervans and motor homes we had used, we knew pretty much exactly what we wanted, and that is also what we would say to anyone: only someone who knows exactly what he wants can custom build his dream camper himself with a little craftsmanship.

One of the first questions around this topic is what purpose the vehicle should have. Will it be used only for camping trips, or should it function for daily use and be a vacation home on wheels? A huge motor home doesn't make sense for daily commuter use, just as a minicamper isn't made to be in the middle of nowhere for weeks on end—it doesn't have the space for the necessary equipment. It's the same for all similar projects: the planning must come first. It all starts with finding out what the requirements for the vehicle are.

After you have decided what the vehicle is to be used for, it's time to add your own wants. In this regard, we had three must-haves: headroom, a big kitchen with a proper fridge, and a cozy interior with a work desk. We were ready to compromise in areas such as the interior bathroom, and a bed conversion to seating was also okay for us. Since we also wanted to be able to park in cities, the vehicle was not allowed to be too long or wide. Because we needed headroom, it was clear to us that we would not be able to use parking garages (pop-tops aren't really our thing), so the height didn't play that big of a role. It turned out to be a 17′5″ long (5.30 m) Opel Movano van with an interior height of 5′11″ (1.80 m)—neither of us are that tall, so we fit standing up—with a kitchen with three burners and a large sink, a household refrigerator with a volume of 3.2 cubic feet (90 liters), which is operated by an inverter, and a bed that can be converted halfway into a table with two benches.

Above: Flying sparks during modifications—Lui's dad cuts off a screw during modifications.
Below: You can also make it through puddles and potholes with front-wheel drive—here, on Malta.

A porta-potty is on board as well as a mobile toilet, and the pump shower can be set up either inside or outside. With the roof box on top, we have seemingly endless storage, which we fill with things such as an inflatable canoe, fishing gear, or a table grill. Because, although our campervan is completely covered with laminate on the inside, we still have—thanks to its short length—enough leeway in terms of weight to be able to take luxury with us.

If the type of vehicle or, even better, the specific model has been figured out, it's time to look at the interior construction. The more inspiration you get from different custom interiors and factory models, the easier it will be for your plans to take final shape. Good planning is extremely important here. There are also great tools on the internet to create 2-D or even 3-D floor plans. Design software such as Sketch-Up and the IKEA Interior Design Planner are great tools to use. If that's too digital for you, break out the pencil and paper or the Legos and build your campervan to scale yourself. In the vehicle, tape markings can also help you get a first feel of the space.

Before we simply start hammering away, we must start planning again. This time, we must plan what will be firmly screwed/glued to the body and where exactly the wiring and water pipes will run. In the end, this should all be nicely hidden behind the paneling. So, where should the supply battery go, and where should the electrical sockets be placed? How will the supply battery be charged? Where do you want to put wiring to the generator and the land hookup? If solar is to be installed on the roof, do you need to plan the roof feed-through? Is 12 volts enough for your appliances, or do you need an inverter to convert the voltage to 230 volts? And when it comes to electricity, safety is very important! Where do fuses belong, and which cable thickness must be chosen for your distances in the vehicle? Get help from a professional if you are not sure.

Now is also the time to consider which energy supplier you'll use to cook, run your heater and boiler, or run your refrigerator or cooler. As soon as gas comes into play, be sure to check the rules and laws and remember your gas detector. By the way, most inspection agencies also give information up front, so you know exactly what to look for. Alternatives to gas can include an alcohol stove or electric cooktops.

Above: Cooking is Steffi's passion—with a three-burner stove, it works great!
Below: A little bit of greenery is also along for the ride, cacti as well as fresh herbs.

Due to the high gas consumption required for heating, we tend to find that independent diesel heaters are definitely the better choice, but that's a matter of taste.

Car bodies tend to be badly insulated. To avoid condensation on the surfaces that will later be clad, insulation must be added. Armaflex® or X-trem Isolator® are widely used for this purpose, both of which are flexible, along with closed-cell insulation materials that were specially developed to prevent condensation. Materials that can absorb moisture—such as glass wool or felt—are not suitable, however. If there is rust or areas with chipped paint, they should be treated before applying the insulation. The insulation is glued directly to the body, and after the insulation has been applied, the car body should no longer be visible anywhere, since that is where cold bridges can occur and build condensation. Whether the floor should also be insulated depends on your individual needs. If there is nothing to be said against reducing the interior height by 1–2 inches, it makes perfect sense to install insulation generously there as well.

Afterward, the paneling can be installed and the furniture can be built. Our campervan is covered completely by laminate, which gives it a cozy feel, holds together well through the interlocking system, and is easily wiped clean, which is definitely a plus for the kitchen. Other than the weight, which is something you should keep an eye on, you need only to watch for sharp splinters in case of an accident.

Space tends to be limited in most campervans, so clever storage techniques really help make the most out of the given space. Attach aluminum foil or other rolls conveniently to a cabinet door and screw the tear-off device to it. Or use rubber bands to fasten objects such as plates in a vertical position. Even professional manufacturers also rely increasingly on creative solutions. How about, for example, magnetic glasses that can also be mounted upside down on the ceiling? We personally swear by fresh herbs in the campervan. Not only are they great in various dishes, but they also smell great in the van and create a homey ambience just by their presence.

Finally, it should be noted that you should not get lost in the details of the modifications, but keep in mind the reason why you are building a campervan in the first place—to travel! So, are you still tinkering around, or have you finally hit the road?

The rear area, *above*, without the bed, and, *below*, the assembled table and half bed

Liguria Sea

SAN MARINO

Florence

San Marino

Ancona

Adriatic Sea

Elba

Gran
Sasso
d'Italia
2,914 ft.

Pescara

Corsica

ROME

Tyrrhenian Sea

of Bonifacio

Sardinia

Sabaudia

Vesuvius
1,277 ft.

Ponza

Pozzuoli

Naples

Ischia

Amalfi
Küste

Capri

0   30 m

Start and Finish
From San Marino to the Amalfi Coast

Distance
389 miles (626 km)

Travel Time
± 9 hours, 15 minutes

Highlights
Rome and the nearby coast
Solfatara Volcano
Hiking along the cliffs of Amalfi

Italy, Including San Marino and Vatican City

THREE COUNTRIES IN ONE,
PLUS A BEAUTIFUL TOUR FROM ROME TO AMALFI

On this trip, we make a special detour on our way to Rome. We don't see much of the border in our campervan—we continue seamlessly up Monte Titano, where at the top San Marino sits on its throne. Luckily, the campground Centro Vacanze San Marino is open year-round, so this is where we park our van in the beginning of January and let ourselves be chauffeured by the public bus up the rest of the way.

Camping Centro Vacanze San Marino
Strada San Michele, 50, San Marino
Phone: +39 0549 90 39 64,
info@centrovacanzesanmarino.com
43°57′34.3″ N, 12°27′40.7″ E

The small country of San Marino has more to offer than its capital of the same name, but we are drawn mostly to the historic center of the town, which sits at the very top of Monte Titano. While we stroll through the streets among the old stone buildings, we realize that there are an extraordinary number of weapons stores. Quick research tells us that in the past, San Marino had a population that placed great value on self-defense, and its inhabitants are still proud of their weapons today. There is probably also a connection there to the three fortresses the city has on display. The three fortresses of Guaita, Cesta, and Montale crown the rocky ridge of Monte Titano, a UNESCO World Heritage Site, and these are the ones to be explored. It is a steep but beautiful path through the nature park up to the top, where a view awaits that stretches west as far as the Apennines and east as far as the Adriatic Sea. The fortresses are connected by an easily accessible path, along which there are plenty of places to stop and rest with seating.

Saubadia beach at sunset

We are sure that the view from here is truly incredible, but the stubborn fog poses a major stumbling block in this department. However, despite the limited visibility, the view from the cable car mountain station down to modern San Mario is terrific.

But San Marino was only a side stop along the way. The actual Italian tour goes from Rome to the Amalfi coast. We are definitely nervous as we approach Rome with our campervan. The traffic must be a nightmare! However, we are pleasantly surprised when, just after exiting the highway, we already find ourselves at the reception counter for the Camping Village Roma. There isn't much going on in January. We look for an open parking spot before we take the bus to the city center.

The free walking tour is too history-heavy for us—we would rather stand with the Romans at the bar in a café and slurp a strong espresso while standing. This way, the drinks cost only half the regular price you would have to pay if you were seated.

Along with the typical sights such as the Colosseum, the Roman Forum, and the Circus Maximus, we also cross the Tiber over the Ponte Sisto and land in the Trastevere neighborhood. Here you can find numerous new modern restaurants with local and international cuisine. We choose the Meccanismo Bistrot, where we order a cold platter as an appetizer and are amazed to see almost all of Italian cuisine served in miniature. Lasagna, pizza, bruschetta, bacon and olive bread, and parmesan croquettes—everything tiny.

And, of course, we also visit the Vatican. We want to visit all countries in Europe, and this mini-country in the middle of the metropolis of Rome is no exception. Standing in St. Peter's Square somehow feels like déjà vu—probably because everyone has seen this place countless times on television. Vatican City is the smallest recognized country in the world, and the 0.2 square miles (0.5 km^2) is quickly explored, especially if you consider that a large part is not open to the public at all.

Camping Village Roma
Via Aurelia, 831, Roma
Phone: +39 06 662 30 18,
roma@humancompany.com
41°53′14.1″ N, 12°24′17.0″ E

Meccanismo Bistrot
Piazza Trilussa, 34, Roma
Phone: +39 06 581 61 11
Monday–Sunday, 7:30 a.m.–2:00 p.m.

Above: Fortress of Guaita—one of three fortresses in San Marino
Below: Who wouldn't recognize it—the Colosseum in Rome

Soon we have seen the eternal city and are being drawn toward the ocean. We take the SS148 going south and turn off in the small town of Sabaudia. At the Agritorismo Fratelli Mizzon, we are the first guests of the year. In a crazy mix of English, a little Italian, and Spanish, we discover from Pietro, the owner of the family-owned business, that the campground has been around for only a year, and they are planning on really expanding it this season.

Agriturismo Fratelli Mizzon
Via S. Andrea, 20A, Sabaudia
Phone: +39 0773 59 30 45,
info@agriturismomizzon.com
41°19′03.2″ N, 13°01′09.8″ E

In a nearby restaurant, we eat delicious pizza for dinner, and the next day we take a little excursion to the beach in Circeo National Park. The coastal dune in the national park, with its characteristic crescent form, stretches from Sabaudia to Capo Portiere, 16 miles (25 km) farther north. Only sand as far as you can see. But if you turn your gaze upward, you will see a completely different natural wonder, the Monte Circeo. The 1,775-foot (541 m) promontory rises majestically at the end of the beach. In the afternoon, we park our campervan at the foot of this very mountain and soon lose the poorly marked hiking trail to its top. Never mind, we think, and make our own way, sometimes steep, up through the forest. A few more circles until we make it, and we stand at the top with a fantastic view of the beach and the village on the other side of the promontory.

Unfortunately, it was hazy and later cloudy as well, or with better visibility we definitely would have been able to see much farther.

After two days in Sabaudia—admittedly, you can spend much longer here—we continue south. We go to Naples, where we park our camper in the suburb of Pozzouli. We check in at the Campeggio Vulcano Solfatara and are amazed to find that we are not just very close to the volcano crater, but rather right in the middle of it! Okay, it stinks tremendously, and even the shower water smells like sulfur, but spending the night in an active volcano crater is worth the stink for us.

The price for the accommodation includes the entrance fee for the whole area, and we can go as often as we want to the hissing and bubbling sites. Unfortunately, the campground is now closed for maintenance, but you can still visit the Solfatara volcano crater. Lightly smelling of sulfur, we get on the bus the following day and later take the train to the center of Naples. A city of light and shadows, there is a lot going on and therefore a lot to see. We stroll through the streets, let ourselves drift a bit, and enjoy the occasional rays of sunshine. It is said that pizza was invented here. We eat it fried for the first time. It tasted good, but somehow we prefer the brick-oven version best.

The last destination on our Italy tour is the Amalfi coast. The route is not the easiest, because towns that are only a few hundred yards from each other as the crow flies are multiple miles away over multiple hundreds of feet of altitude with the campervan. Because we don't like to drive through narrow streets with our van, and there is a small parking problem in Amalfi, we decide to stay at the Campeggio Ostello Beata Solitudo di Paolo Genova in Agerola, above the cliffs. The entrance to the campground is luckily not as complicated as its name, and soon after we arrive at the gate, Paolo also arrives on his bicycle. He places us in the somewhat chaotic backyard of the property and immediately starts raving about his beautiful Amalfi coast. He also gives us the tip to stop by a local cheese dairy and to try the *fiori di latte*. Right after our siesta, that was the first place we went, and the very light mozzarella-like cheese tasted so delicious that we took some back with us.

In addition, Paolo recommended the stairs down to Amalfi. The next morning, we leave well equipped from the center of the village, following the Via A. Coppola toward the coast, turn on the Via Miramare, and find the beginning of the stairs on the left side after the Pizzeria Leonardo. The views along the way are incredible—the ocean shines below us in turquoise, and, warmed by the sun, we descend step by step through the springtime surroundings. The whole route is marked with a white-red symbol. We follow this old mule trail for a good two thousand steps, until we finally arrive in Amalfi. We covered a height of 2,073 feet (632 m) in about an hour and a half and are very happy that after we tour the city, a bus will take us back to Agerola. But first, there is delicious pizza, and because the day is so beautiful, a gelati at the harbor. Ultimately, this is the end of our tour through Italy. We will continue to Ancona and, from there, to Croatia with the ferry.

Caseificio La Montanina
Piazza Generale Avitabile, 3, Pianillo
The delicious cheese of the cheese dairy is called fiori di latte and can be tasted on-site.

Previous double page: Lui at a Sabaudia beach in Circeo National Park
Above: The buildings in Naples are all black—probably from the exhaust . . .
Below: Beautiful Amalfi—our hiking destination after around two thousand steps

0

BOSNIA
AND
HERZEGOVINA

Pag

Zadar

Knin

Dugi
Otok

Troglav
1,913 ft.

Krka National
Park

Šibenik

Primošten

Adriatic Sea

Trogir

Split

Omis

Brač

Makarska

Hvar

Vis

Korčula

Mali Ston

Mljet

Dubrovnik

Start and Finish
From Split to Dubrovnik

Distance
284 miles (457 km)

Travel Time
± 7 hours, 20 minutes

Highlights
Split
Krka National Park
Jadranska Magistrala seaside drive

Croatia

FROM SPLIT VIA KRKA NATIONAL PARK TO DUBROVNIK
ALONG THE JADRANSKA MAGISTRALA

We leave the ferry named *Dubrovnik*, which took us from Ancona to Croatia overnight, well rested and recovered. First, we go to the market and have breakfast there—it is still too early to check in anywhere. Around midday, we park our campervan at Camping Stobreč Split right at the water. At this time of year, such a parking spot doesn't even cost extra, and they are also available without a reservation.

Camping Stobreč Split
Sv. Lovre 6, Split
Phone: +385 21 32 54 26,
camping.split@gmail.com
43°30′14.2″ N, 16°31′35.5″ E

The next day, we venture into the center of Split, but this time with a public bus. We stroll through the narrow streets, discover Diocletian's Palace, and land at the harbor promenade amid the hustle and bustle of the fresh-produce market at Stari Pazar, which is open daily starting at 6:30 a.m. Fruits, vegetables, and homemade specialties are offered for sale. The little Café Bile at the edge of the market square on the Stari Pazar attracts our attention. It is well visited by the locals, who eat delicious-looking dishes. We want to as well and resort to gestures and hand signs to order, since no one here speaks English. While the *cevapcici* are sizzling—they will be served to us later in a burger bun—fries are made from raw potatoes right before our eyes! The food is very delicious and very inexpensive. Whoever likes their Croatian cuisine a little more sophisticated than at a local food stand will be happy at Konoba Fetivi.

Café Bile
Stari Pazar, Split
Croatian fast food, freshly prepared
and original

View down upon the old city of Dubrovnik

That is where we eat on our second evening in Split. The menu is small—there is primarily fresh-caught fish—but all the Croatian classics can be found there as well.

Konoba Fetivi
Tomica Stine 4, Split
Tuesday–Sunday, 12:00 p.m.–11:00 p.m.
Croatian specialties, mostly fish

About thirty minutes away from Split lies Trogir. The whole old city is a UNESCO World Heritage Site and can be reached only by a stone bridge—so, a small, offshore island. We park our van on the mainland and go by foot to the city center: a very impressive location with twisting alleys and beautiful buildings. A bus and a ship line travel from Split to Trogir in case you don't want to drive there yourself.

We continue driving along in the afternoon, and we immediately notice the next small island in the middle of the turquoise sea a little off the road: Primošten. Of course, we want to go there, so we turn around and park right on the beach promenade. Visitors can enter Primošten only by foot. First, we discover the port with the small fishing boats that look like they're floating in air—the water

is so clear. Then it's off into the labyrinth of alleyways until we reach the top of the hill near a small church. We enjoy the view and slowly make our way back. Along the way, we treat ourselves to a spinach-filled *burek*, a delicious Croatian baked specialty. Only now do we notice the beautiful beaches located on both sides of the Primošten access bridge. If only the temperatures would also invite us to swim—it's a true paradise!

After arriving in Krka National Park, it is already late afternoon, and we park at a small campground in Lozovac—the only one in the region that accepts visitors at this time of year. The circular hiking trail of Skradinski Buk is probably known to all visitors of the Krka National Park. You park far up, and the hikers go the narrow way up to the beginning of the actual trail on foot. If you are here during the main season, you can also take the park bus. The over-1-mile (almost 2 km) circular trail leads over beautifully constructed footbridges. It goes through the forest and on footbridges over water rapids before reaching the big waterfall. The nature is great, and in the middle of the winter, when we are there, the trail is of course pleasantly uncrowded.

Much less known is the viewing platform next to Roski Slap in the northern part of Krka National Park.

Above: On the way into Krka National Park
Below: One of the many waterfalls in Krka National Park on the Skradinski Buk circuit

Roski Slap (*slap* means waterfall), which flows from Visovac Lake, is worth a visit, most importantly the view from the viewing platform right next to it. Behind the national park hut, a trail leads steeply up the rocks. Appropriate shoes are highly recommended for the short stretch. Handles are partially available when the trail goes up the boulders too steeply. Once you arrive at the top, the view over the lake embedded between two rock faces and beyond is revealed.

Hiking in Krka National Park
Skrandinski Buk circuit hiking trail
A 1.2-mile (2 km) route on footbridges over the waterfalls and through the forest, very busy in the main season, includes a swimming location.

Roski Slap
Short but very steep hiking trail to a viewing platform with views over the Krka National Park

---

From Krka National Park, we drive back south and now follow the Jadranska Magistrala, one of the most beautiful coastal routes in Europe. Actually, this route begins in Trieste, Italy, and ends in Ulcinj, Montenegro. We go only the partial route from Šibenik to Dubrovnik, on the stretch called the D8. The street almost always leads directly along the ocean, which allows us fantastic views of the Croatian coast with its turquoise waters and white-pebble beaches. Once we reach Zaton Doli, we turn on the D414 and reach Ston and Mali Ston. These two towns are located on the Pelješac Peninsula and form the longest fortress system in Europe! This wall is an unbelievable 3.4 miles long (5.5 km), putting it in second place worldwide behind the Great Wall of China. Of course, we want to see this highlight with our own eyes, so we park in Ston and go directly to the wall. A terrific experience.

The campsite Solitudo Sunny is still closed, so we park ourselves in front of it for the night. The next day, we take the bus into the historic downtown of Dubrovnik. This sector is surrounded by massive city walls, upon which you can walk around Dubrovnik for a handsome fee. In general, we notice that inside the walls, the prices are much more expensive than what you find otherwise in Croatia. Dubrovnik is becoming an island of high prices thanks to the many cruise ships and other tourists. Even so, the old city is impressively beautiful, and film lovers are constantly amazed to find locations from well-known flicks. For us, however, a slightly bitter taste from Dubrovnik remains, because here you can see the negative effects of excessive tourism all too clearly.

Above: Market stand at the Stari Pazar fresh market in Split
Below: View to Primošten—a beautiful, small island town

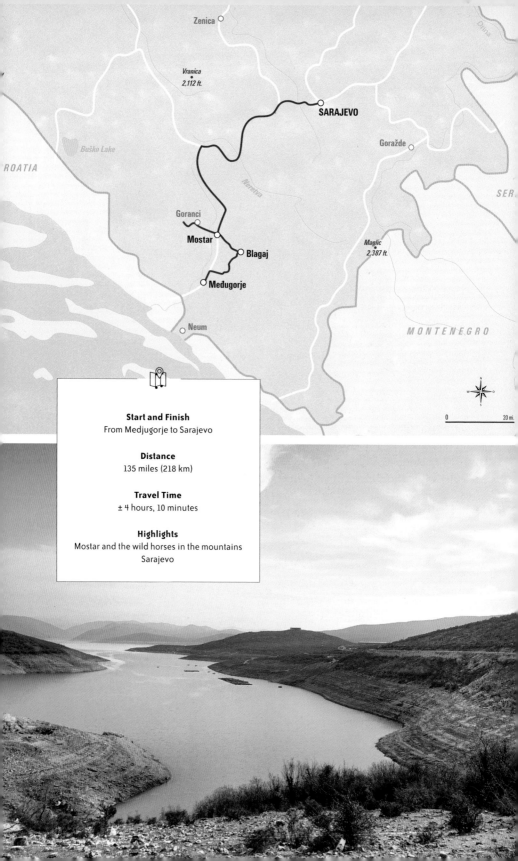

Zenica

Vranica
2,112 ft.

SARAJEVO

Goražde

Buško Lake

CROATIA

SER.

Neretva

Goranci

Mostar

Maglic
2,387 ft.

Blagaj

Međugorje

Neum

MONTENEGRO

N
W — O
S

0   20 mi.

Start and Finish
From Međugorje to Sarajevo

Distance
135 miles (218 km)

Travel Time
± 4 hours, 10 minutes

Highlights
Mostar and the wild horses in the mountains
Sarajevo

Bosnia and Herzegovina

OVER THE FAMOUS MOSTAR BRIDGE INTO SARAJEVO,
THE CITY OF TWO WORLDS

The coast of Bosnia and Herzegovina, which splits Croatia into two parts, is just 12 miles long (20 km). That is where we cross the border into the country, and after a quick look at our green insurance card, the customs agents let us pass. We do a quick exchange of euros into convertible marks—we had already researched the rates online—and the trip began.

In Blagaj, we find a spot at Camping Mali Wimbledon. The campground is located around the home of the owners, and a toilet and a shower are cleaned for us in no time. In the afternoon, we take a walk to the Buna River Spring, which is regarded as one of the most beautiful karst springs in Europe, and we eat a small bite in the restaurant directly on the Buna, while we marvel at the Muslim Dervish monastery Blagaj Tekija on the other side of the river.

Encouraged by Ibro, the campground owner, we take the public bus the next day from Blagaj into Mostar. The approximately twenty-five-minute bus ride is, as expected,

not too comfortable, but very exciting. After arriving in the center of Mostar, we stroll through the streets, pass the souvenir shops, and finally arrive at the famous bridge Stari Most, the namesake of Mostar. It was completely destroyed in the Croat-Bosniak War, but since 2004 it has been restored to its original design from its own rubble and is now the city's landmark. In the summer, young men jump bravely from the bridge for a few coins into the flowing Neretva River below, but during our trip there is nothing to be seen of that. Instead, we hear unfamiliar sounds when we cross the bridge—the muezzin calls to prayer, and we quickly discover the mosque as well, which we are quick to explore.

Camping Mali Wimbledon
Blagaj BB, Mostar
Phone: +387 36 57 25 82, ibrozalihic@hotmail.com
Open all year
43°15'47.4" N, 17°52'40.5" E

Man-made Bileća Lake on the roadside in the
Republic of Srpska

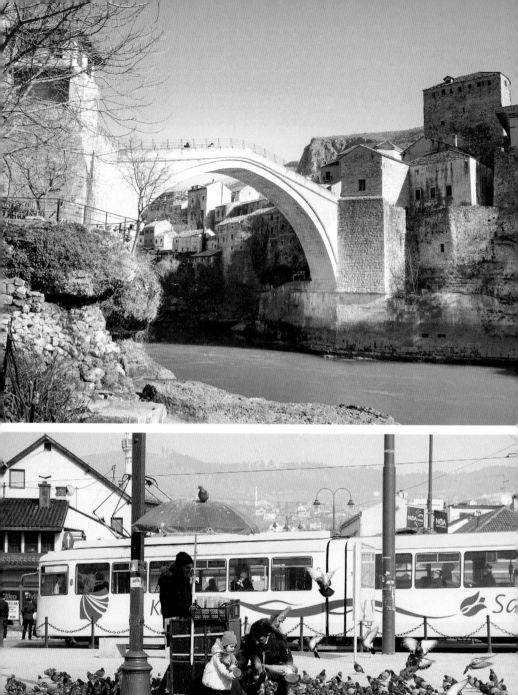

In Restoran Šadrvan, we eat a typical local lunch, but not without being watched by cats, which roam about everywhere.

We were introduced to Mirjana through friends in Switzerland. She lives in Mostar and knows where the wild horses live in the mountains around Mostar. Without any hesitation, she packs us, her son, and her father—the only one who speaks a language we are familiar with, a little French—into her car. Near Goranci, far from everything, we get out and start our search. Right when we are about to give up, we discover something. It wasn't we who discovered the horses, but rather the horses who noticed us. In the winter, many residents come here and bring the horses something to eat—Mirjana naturally thought of this as well and takes bread out of a rustling bag. And so, the horses trot up to us with their foals—some of them even let us pet them. Wild horses . . . well, let's just say horses that live in the wild—Steffi is definitely in seventh heaven!

But the true highlight of our Bosnia and Herzegovina trip begins only just now. We drive to Sarajevo. In the borough of Ilidža, there are campgrounds, but they are still closed. So, we rent an apartment and stay a whole week. During a free walking tour, Enes tells us a lot about the time during the war, but also how residents live today, and that especially the youth, like himself, want to bring their Sarajevo back to life.

Of course, you still see the past. Bullet holes in the facades and red roses drawn everyplace where more than three people were killed in grenade attacks are wartime witnesses that are still present.

Wild Horse Location
There is a waterhole here, where horses are seen frequently.
43°25′36.2″ N, 17°40′20.1″ E
Careful: There are still plenty of landmines in Bosnia, so please stay on the paths!

Restoran Šadrvan
Jusovina 11, Mostar
Phone: +387 36 57 80 95
Open daily from 9:00 a.m. to 11:00 p.m.

Camping Sarajevo
Mratnjevaće 57, Sarajevo-Ilidza
Phone: +387 33 76 35 65,
info@camping-sarajevo.com
Open March 1–November 1
43°50′20.0″ N, 18°15′52.7″ E

Above: The famous bridge Stari Most, the namesake of Mostar, has been put back into one piece.
Below: Pigeons are probably fed all around the world—like here in Sarajevo.

But Sarajevo has much more to offer! On Ferhadija Street, at the Sarajevo Meeting of Cultures point, the architecture of the Austro-Hungarian rule with its Vienna-like buildings meets buildings from the Ottoman period. This contrast goes so far that no alcohol is served in the Ottoman part, while it's easily accessible in the rest of Sarajevo.

We wind our way through the narrow streets until we reach Baščaršija Square and eat *burek* (pastries filled with either ground beef, spinach, or potatoes) in the Buregdžinica Bosna restaurant with the typical yogurt drink and stroll through Coppersmith's Street (Kazandžiluk in Bosnian), where we marvel at the craftsmanship. Later, we climb the Yellow Bastion on foot (Žuta Tabija in Bosnian)—and look down on the 291,000 city residents. There we notice the many minarets.

Before we leave the city, we drive to the Tunnel of Hope. For a small fee, we are able to learn everything about the famous supply tunnel during the siege of Sarajevo from 1992 to 1995, which supplied the surrounded population in the heart of the city with food and medicine.

Something we didn't know during our visit, but what is now clear after visiting forty-five European countries and making countless city trips: for us, Sarajevo is one of the top three most-exciting and worth-visiting cities in Europe. So, if you ever get the chance, definitely make the trip and experience this gem of history and blending of cultures in person.

Caffe Tito
Zmaja od Bosne 5, Sarajevo
Open daily from 8:00 a.m. to midnight

Buregdžinica Bosna
Bravadžiluk 11, Sarajevo
Open daily from 8:00 a.m. to 11:00 p.m.

Top left: Wild horses in the mountains near Mostar
Top right: Bosnian coffee—similar to the Turkish sort
Below: Ottoman part of Sarajevo

0   30 mi.

BOSNIA AND
HERZEGOVINA

SERBIA

Pljevlja

Durmitor
National   Žabljak
Park

Mojkovac

Bijelo
Polje

Niksić

Berane

KOSOVO

Vilusi

ceg-
Novi

Kotor
Sveti
Stefan

PODGORICA

ALBANIA

Budva
Petrovac

Virpazar

Skadarsee

Drin

Tara

Start and Finish
From Herceg Novi to Durmitor National Park

Distance
193 miles (310 km)

Travel Time
± 5 hours, 50 minutes

Highlights
Coastal villages
Virpazar
Tara River Canyon
Durmitor National Park

comewith

Montenegro

ALONG THE COAST WITH CHORES ON LAKE SHKODËR
TO DURMITOR NATIONAL PARK

Montenegro is one of the few countries that are not members of the EU but have the euro as their currency. So, it wasn't a surprise that the fee required shortly after crossing the border is in euros. We don't know what the five euros are for, but we pay it anyway.

The first stop is Herceg Novi, a small city on the northern coast of Montenegro. Because today is Sunday, we can park for free. During the main travel season, it is recommended to keep a lookout for an open parking spot long before reaching the city.

The town itself is not very large and is perfect to explore on foot. We climb the stairs of the old fortress up to the Church of Saint Michael the Archangel. From up here, the view across the bay is beautiful. We go through the narrow street, pass a gate, and are standing at the main square just a few steps later. A look back shows us what we just walked through. A beautiful clock tower, surrounded by beautiful old buildings—Herceg Novi is truly a feast for the eyes. A few winding streets later, we are standing at the small harbor, sit down in a café, and enjoy the day to its fullest.

We can take the ferry to get to Kotor, but we decide to make the journey by land. The road is partly littered with large, deep holes, but the views of the two islets of Gospa od Škrpjela and Sveti Đorđe as well as the waterfall Orijenski Vodopad near Risan are enough compensation for the extra effort. Having arrived in Kotor, we look at the tourist information in the small building near the entrance gate to the old city and get ourselves a city map. The lady tells us that a carnival parade starts in two hours. We want to look at the city by the time the parade starts. We quickly pass through the entrance gate and find ourselves among stone houses with only narrow alleys between, and small shops are everywhere.

Above: We drive through the Tara River Canyon to Durmitor National Park.
Below: There's a watchdog on site at the Camping Maslina.

The old city is so small, you don't need an exact route to get through it—just start walking. We are impressed by the stately Saint Tryphon Cathedral, behind which the rock face shoots up immediately, where the small fortress of San Giovanni is perched on top. A trail around 2.8 miles long (4.5 km) runs along the city walls and leads visitors to the fortress. The view is supposed to be fantastic when the weather is good, but that's not the case for us.

The carnival parade turns out to be a children's parade, and apart from dozens of cheerleaders and sailors there is not much to see, not even confetti. Yes, we are used to a different kind of carnival.

Kotor itself is a beautiful, unassuming, and small town with an old city absolutely worth seeing. We don't even want to imagine this small gem when the huge cruise ships are anchored at the harbor with thousands of passengers flooding the streets. Especially then, as in so many other cases: the earlier you are there, the better.

Unfortunately, all the campgrounds in Kotor are still closed, and even a hotel with a parking spot for our campervan cannot be found (it is pretty tall, with a roof of 10 feet [3 m]). So, we are forced to drive farther and spend the night in Budva.

We first visit Budva the next day. On one hand, there are modern skyscrapers and big hotels, but on the other hand it has a small old city with typical stone buildings. That is what draws us, and we stroll through narrow streets once again to reach the citadel. Budva, in contrast to Kotor, lies right on the ocean, and that gives the city a very different flair. We visit the former fort, which has not only exhibitions worth a visit, but also terrific views from the terrace out to sea, over the city, and to the hills behind it. Even though the contrasts between old and new Budva are large, we find that this visit was really worth it.

On the other hand, we are rather disappointed by our next destination. We drive south along the coast and reach Sveti Stefan. We heard a lot about the small island, and admittedly it does look wonderful from the road. But no one told us that only residents are allowed to access it, and we were of course disappointed when we were turned back by the gatekeeper.

Above: Sveti Stefan—unfortunately, no access for visitors
Below: Crno Jezero—also known as Black Lake—in Durmitor National Park

Restaurant Galija
Buljarica BB, Kalud-erac, Petrovac
Phone: +382 33 46 17 17
Open daily from 8:00 a.m. to 11:00 p.m.
Seafood and traditional cuisine

Camping Maslina
Buljarica BB, Petrovac
Phone: +382 68 60 20 40,
camping.mne@gmail.com
Open all year
42°11'52.3" N, 18°57'55.7" E

In Petrovac na Moru, we finally find an open campground at Camping Maslina. We park here a few days and enjoy the proximity to the ocean and the culinary arts presented at Restaurant Galija, which is along the beach. We want to learn more about the country and its people, so we decide to do some work and travel in Virpazar on Lake Shkodër. A British family runs a small guesthouse here and needs some help preparing the house and garden for the coming season. Emma and Ben have been living in Montenegro for over ten years, and their three children go to the public school here.

View to Virpazar on Lake Shkodër

They explain to us that there isn't a single recycling station with trash separation in the country, and that many buildings there—even in nature conservation zones such as Lake Shkodër—are able to be constructed only because of corrupt officials. Even so, Montenegro is a land worth living in, and they enjoy their personal paradise here.

Of course, we also explore the region and go on many hikes; for example, to Godinje. First, we follow the road from Virpazar to Bar and turn left behind the church down the beaten path. Starting here, the hiking trail is marked, and it first leads through the forest and later up to the top of the hill. It continues through a valley to Godinje, where Misko—a friend of our host—tells us more about the small village while we sip on his wine. At dusk, we make our way back along the street on the banks of Lake Shkodër.

Winery Garnet—Misko Lekovic
Godinje, Virpazar
Phone: +382 67 35 55 35,
www.winerygarnet.com
Wine tastings with local specialties and tours
in English upon request

After our stay with Emma and Ben, we continue on to Albania, but a few months later we visited Montenegro again in the backcountry, and since these destinations can be connected well with the coastal trip, we will tell you about them here.

The E64 leads inland, and at Mojkovac we turn on to the P4, which follows the Tara River through a narrow gorge. First, at the Most na Đurđevića Tara bridge—you can fly over the river on a zip line here—we turn left on the P5 and drive into Durmitor National Park. We check in at the Auto Camp Razvršje on the outskirts of Žabljak. From here, we start the hike to Crno Jezero, the Black Lake, the next day. This glacial lake breaks down into two parts and lies at an elevation of 4,646 feet (1,416 m). We circle the two lakes and enjoy the day in the middle of this wonderful part of nature.

Montenegro has very beautiful cities along the coast, but there is also a lot of tourism there. If you are looking for a more low-key experience, you can find endless expanses and deserted plains in Durmitor National Park. And another good thing: the country is not very big—you can cross relatively quickly from one end to the other.

Auto Camp Razvršje
Razvršje 66, Žabljak
Phone: +382 67 44 44 77,
mdurmitor@gmail.com
Open all year
43°08'40.6" N, 19°06'46.6" E

Above: Inner city of Kotor—a very beautiful place
Below: Church of Michael the Archangel in Herceg Novi—beautiful view from there

MONTENEGRO

KOSOVO

Skutarisee

Drin

Shkodër

Kukës

Black Drin

Mt. Korab
9,068 ft.

NORTH
MACEDONIA

Durrës

TIRANA

Camping Pa Emer

Elbasan

Shkumbin

Lushnjë

Pogradec

Lake
Prespa

Seman

Vlorë

Vjosa

Radhimë Beach

Llogara Pass

Gjirokastër

A d r i a t i c   S e a

GREECE

Sarandë

The Blue Eye

Ksamil

30 mi.

Start and Finish
From Shkodër to Gjirokaster

Distance
278 miles (448 km)

Travel Time
± 8 hours, 45 minutes

Highlights
Camping Pa Emer
Llogara Pass
Butrint and Gjirokaster

Albania

CONTRARY TO ALL PRECONCEPTIONS FROM THE NORTH
ALL THE WAY INTO THE SOUTH

Starting in Montenegro, we circle Lake Shkodër and cross the border into Albania with a lake view. At customs, immense chaos reigns. Tractor trailers are parked everywhere and in all different directions, and we barely make it through between them. The border officials greet us with a smile—maybe Albania won't be as bad as we thought?

Our first destination is Shkodër—there we have already picked out a rest spot. But first, we have to drive completely through the city. No one pays any attention to traffic laws: pedestrians are walking in the streets along with dogs, donkey carts, and merchants selling live fish. Yes, Shkodër overwhelms us a bit in the beginning. So many impressions—everything is different from just a short while back in Montenegro. Luckily, the rest stop is open, so we park our campervan and go back by foot to the center. Romany boys drive scraps around on ancient mopeds, and a few streets later we pass by their settlement: some

corrugated-metal huts with a lot of trash lying around and kids playing in the middle of it all. We find a bakery a little farther along and marvel at the bread selection! With kernels, light, dark, round, or long—it's almost like home, and we haven't been home in months! Of course, we take advantage and have already bitten into the rolls as we exit. We also see beautiful mosques and watch the street merchants. We eat our dinner at the restaurant at the rest stop. The appetizer, two main courses, and a dessert, with beer and wine, cost us only eleven euros, including a large tip, and it was really delicious!

Camping & Restaurant Legjenda,
Agron 1, Shkodër
Phone: +355 69 650 67 46,
info@campinglegjenda.com
Open all year
42°02′37.0″ N, 19°29′20.9″ E

Above: Road users in Albania move along carelessly.
Below: Castle garden of the Kalaja Fortress with a view of the surrounding mountains

The next day, we make our way by foot to Rozafa Castle, which is perched on a hill over Shkodër. Up here it is quiet—the hectic city is far away, and that gives us the chance to view the city from a certain distance. It is massive, and the view goes much farther. Below, the contrasts couldn't be any greater. Next to a modern skyscraper lies a Romany settlement; a big Mercedes-Benz sedan drives behind a horse cart, and while some people come out of the supermarket with full bags, others are searching through the trash for leftovers. The massive contrasts really make us think, and we can recommend to anyone traveling to Albania to spend enough time here in order to be able to process this culture shock in peace.

We continue to Durrës, the largest port city in the country. Camping Pa Emer lies a little south of the city, which means "that with no name," which is very strange, considering pretty much everyone traveling to Albania knows this place! Parking spots directly on the ocean, a small island right off the coast, and the elderly owner couple, who will also cook upon request.

The next day we meet an acquaintance in Durrës, and she shows us the city. A Greek amphitheater, parts of the old city wall, and a modern indoor swimming pool above the beach—Durrës has a lot of things, except

maybe a lot of charm. We chat away, and it's already dusk by the time we make our way back to the campground. Driving in Albania is already difficult in daylight because of all the holes in the pavement, the animals and the people on the road, and the wild passing maneuvers, but at night, there is the additional challenge of the unlit road users. After the half-hour drive, including a near accident, we fall into bed and enjoy the next day on the beautiful beach in front of our campervan.

The national highway SH8 brings us into the south. We spend the night in Radhimë at a simple parking spot directly on the water before we travel up the Llogara Pass the next day. When the weather is good, we should be able to see all the way to Greece at the top of the pass. We meander our way past countless potholes and a few cows as we slowly ascend the serpentine roads. Our campervan makes it over the crest effortlessly at a height of 3,369 feet (1,027 m) above sea level—and the south of Albania stretches before us.

Camping Pa Emer
Rrakull Karpen, Kavaja
Phone: +355 664 15 15 02,
reservation@kampingpaemer.com
Open all year
41°10′55.8″ N, 19°28′41.8″ E

Above: Within Castle Rozafa by Shkodër
Below: Our parking spot directly on the water at Camping Pa Emer
Following double page: Bird's-eye view of the "Blue Eye" lake

Sandy beaches as far as the eye can see, turquoise waters, and what is that? That must be Corfu, the Greek island! Amazing! The drive down the southern side is no less impressive. We enjoy the terrific views of the most-beautiful beaches in Albania, but we also discover small concrete structures. They are old bunker constructions, hundreds of which were built at places of strategic importance across the whole country but are falling apart today.

After arriving at the bottom, we drive along the long sandy beaches and see the ocean transition from turquoise to blue up close. The first beaches are remote, with the later ones approaching civilization. Unfortunately, the beaches are not excluded from the trash problems in the country, with a lot of plastic garbage lying around. Life is simple: the people are unbelievably hospitable and helpful. With each mile traveled, our respect for the unfamiliar country grows more and more, our curiosity and spirit of discovery even more so.

As far as hospitality goes, no one can hold a candle to the owners of Ksamil Camping. We are warmly welcomed and assigned a place in the front yard of the house. They spoil us daily with coffee and tea specialties—sometimes there are also traditional baked goods and of course fresh flowers. The campground offers full infrastructure, and the town of Ksamil is the perfect starting point for diverse places worth seeing in the surrounding area. We stay a whole week and go on various excursions. One is Sarandë, a small port city with Mediterranean flair on the water and typical Albanian hecticness in the city center.

Camping Caravan Ksamil
Parku Kombëtar i Butrintit, SH81, Ksamil
Phone: +355 694 26 36 97
alekcerro@yahoo.com
Open all year
39°46'41.3" N, 20°00'21.3" E

We park our camper somewhere on the side of the road and go on foot into the hustle and bustle. Women carry cloths full of vegetables through the alleys, while some men stand on the sidewalk, all of them holding thick bundles of money, seemingly operating mobile exchange offices. The entire range of Mercedes-Benz vehicles, from old to brand new, pushes its way between small trucks through the streets. It is a little more peaceful at the harbor, and we are drawn to a restaurant where we try typical fish dishes. Later we go to Kalaja e Lëkurësit castle, which lies on the hill behind the city. From here we can see Corfu even better, especially since we are now at the same altitude as the Greek island, and tour boats leave Sarandë to go over to Corfu.

Restaurant Limani
Lagjia Nr.1, Rruga Jonianet 3, Sarandë
Phone: +355 85 22 58 58,
limanibbsarande@gmail.com
Open daily from 7:15 a.m. to 12:45 a.m.
39°52'25.1" N, 20°00'30.3" E

Much more interesting ruins can be found 2.5 miles (4 km) south of Ksamil at the UNESCO World Heritage Site of Butrint. The antique dig site is located at Lake Butrint and was discovered by Italian archeologists in 1928. We stroll through the extensive grounds, marvel at the structures, and enjoy the warm spring day.

On the way to Gijrokastër, our next destination, we turn left from the SH99 onto a farm road in the middle of the Mali i Gjerë mountains, pay a few lek (the Albanian currency), and park our campervan at the end of the dirt road. We walk a few yards by foot until we have arrived at the "Blue Eye" lake, or, in Albanian, Syri i Kaltër. The Blue Eye is a karst spring that emits 6,000 liters of water per second out of the ground and has an unbelievable deep-blue color. A somewhat wobbly platform offers a view from above, so that we can really see the Blue Eye.

From the Blue Eye lake, we travel farther along the SH99 deep into the backcountry until it joins the SH78. These mountains! We

are astonished, even though we know that the Balkans take their name from the mountains of the same name. We check into a small family campground a little outside Gijrokastër. It is already late morning as we take a stroll into the historic center. Gijrokastër was threatened to almost become a ghost town, until UNESCO named it a World Heritage Site in 2005 and increased tourism stimulated the economy. The town captivates through its unique architecture—the roofs of all the buildings are covered with slate plates. We make our way through the alleys up to Gijrokastër Fortress. Along with the military museum inside, the outside area is also very beautiful, where a famous plane wreck can be found. The distant view of the mountains is also terrific.

In the evening there is a schnapps tasting at the campground, including homemade Albanian specialties. A fitting end to our Albanian trip before we travel through the mountains to Greece.

Camping Gjirokaster
Rruga Valere, Topullaraj, Gjirokaster
Phone: +355 69 839 14 92,
info@campinggjirokaster.al
Open all year
40°06'06.6" N, 20°09'02.3" E

Top left: Fish for lunch in Sarandë
Middle: Plane wreck in Gjirokaster
Top right: Daily indulgence at Camping Ksamil
Below: View of the harbor in Sarandë

ALBANIA

Thessaloniki
Chalkidiki
Thasos

Mt. Smolikas
8,652 ft.

Vikos

Mt. Olympus
9,570 ft.

Mt. Athos
6,670 ft.

Corfu

Ioannina

Meteora
Klöster

Larissa

Aegean

Volos

Camping Sikia

Haliacmon

Pineios

Ionian

Sea

Achelous

Lefkada

Leukas

Delphi

Euboea

Skyros

Sea

Ler

Cephalonia

Patras

Hosios
Loukas

Chalcis

Andros

Zakynthos

Peloponnese

Corinth

Athens

Piraeus

Mediterranean

Nafplio

Kea

Sea

Kalamäta

Sparta

Leonidio

Monemvasia

Milos

Start and Finish
From the Vikos Gorge up to the Pelion

Distance
1,107 miles (1,781 km)

Travel Time
± 25 hours, 30 minutes

Highlights
Meteora, Lefkada, Mystras, Monemvasia
Easter in Leonidio

30 mi.

Greece

HIGHLIGHTS ON THE MAINLAND, INCLUDING THE PELOPONNESE

Coming from Albania, we are very excited to see the good condition of the E853 in Greece, which we follow until Kalkati. From there, we take back roads to Monodendri. We want to go to the Vikos Gorge in the Pindus Mountains. There are different viewing points, but we are heading for the Oxya viewpoint. A few vehicles can be parked at the end of the road, and the last few yards can be done on foot. Just a few more steps around a boulder, and wow, the view is spectacular! In front of us there is a steep, 100-yard drop down into the Vikos Gorge. The gorge is not wide, but very deep—so deep that it made it into the *Guinness Book of World Records*, because relative to its width, it is the deepest gorge in the world. You can even descend into the gorge and hike through it. The trail starts near the Agia Paraskevi Monastery and leads approximately 2,625 feet (800 m) down a set of stairs into the Vikos Gorge.

We drive through the hilly landscape farther south to Ioannina, where we find a

spot at Camping Limnopoula directly on the lake. We stay here a few days, enjoy the good weather, and eat our first and at the same time the best gyros/pita in all of Greece in the local restaurant Oivlaxoi.

In Greece, tolls are measured by vehicle height at the front axle. With our boxy van, its quickly becomes pretty expensive, so we decide to avoid toll roads as much as possible.

Camping Limnopoula
Kanari 10, Ioannina
Phone: +30 26510 252 65,
noioanninon@hotmail.gr
Open all year
39°40'40.1" N, 20°50'37.9" E

Restaurant Oivlaxoi
Mitropoleos 3, Ioannina
Phone: +30 26510 700 21
Open daily from 12:00 p.m. to 1:00 a.m.
39°40'07.0" N, 20°51'23.5" E

Monmemvasia—the small, beautiful island directly off the coast

Because of this, we don't take the A2 to Meteora, but the somewhat windier E92. From a distance, we already see the typical rock formations of the region and finally the first monastery as well. We travel between the rock formations via Kastraki to the monastery buildings, which are perched at the tops. At one point in history, there were twenty-four monasteries, but today only six of them are occupied and able to be visited, of which two are women's convents and the rest are occupied by men. We view each of them from the outside and go inside two of them. For this, Steffi must borrow a wraparound skirt, because the monasteries allow only female visitors wearing skirts and men in long pants. The views from up here are terrific—the buildings, including the grounds, are well cared for and beautiful, and inside there are exciting exhibitions to visit as well.

We spend the night at Camping Vrachos Kastraki, where we also we also go on a hike.

By now, we have dedicated enough time to the Pindus mountain range and its hidden treasures, and now it's time to drive to the ocean. Visiting islands with the camper normally includes fares for the ferry, but not Lefkada. So, we drive southwest and reach the island of Lefkada over a dam. We use the campground at Desimi Beach as a home base: a small, simple campground that surrounds a bay. We park directly at the water and enjoy the April sun before we explore the island in the coming days.

The most-beautiful beaches are on the western coast. We visit Egremni Beach, but due to road construction we can marvel at it only from above. The snow-white sand forms a barrier between the turquoise waters and the steep towering rocks of the coast. We follow the road far into the south of Lefkada, where a lighthouse stands on Doucato Cape. Far in the north of the western coast is Kathisma Beach, which is the most well-known beach on the island.

Campsite Vrachos Kastraki
Kalambaka 422 00, Greece
Phone: +30 24320 222 93,
www.campingkastraki.com
Open all year
39°42′47.8″ N, 21°36′56.5″ E

Camping Desimi Beach
Kavvadas Bros, Vlycho, Lefkada
Phone: +30 6937 33 42 40,
camping.desimi@gmail.com
Open all year
38°40′21.2″ N, 20°42′39.0″ E

Above: The monasteries of Meteora crown the rocky peaks.
Below: Our parking spot at Camping Limnopoula on Lake Pamvotida

We leave Lefkada after a few days and drive along the Gulf of Corinth to Delphi. Along the way, we help a few turtles cross the street safely—we call them Greek emergencies— and marvel at the beautiful colors of the ocean and the landscape on the route.

We plan on looking at the Delphi dig site tomorrow—today we are still enjoying the unique views of the olive groves out to the sea that we have from our spot at the Delphi campground. Delphi was the seat of the most important oracle of the ancient Greek world and was considered the center of the world for a long time. We arrive at the dig site early and are impressed at how such structures could be built using such simple resources.

Camping Delphi
4th km Delphi, Chrisso road, Delphi
Phone: +30 22650 822 09,
info@delphicamping.com
Open from April 1 to October 31

38°28'43.1" N, 22°28'25.7" E

That afternoon, we drive to the Hosios Loukas Monastery, located only 22 miles (36 km) east of Delphi. Nestled among nature with great views, the monastery extends over several buildings. We explore the grounds, the old stables, the *fotanama* (a room with a fireplace and stone benches along the walls), and finally, of course, the old and the somewhat-newer church. We especially enjoy the mosaics covered in gold.

After the short pit stop, the journey continues directly to the Corinth Canal. Today the canal is almost exclusively used by recreational boaters because it is too narrow for large ships. But the dead-straight line of it paired with the turquoise sea is already an amazing visual. We enjoy the view and then drive to the northern side of the canal to the tip, where an imposing lighthouse stands at Cape Melagavi. Along the way we pass a lagoon, which is affectionately called a "lake" by the inhabitants but contains salt water. On the shore is a large parking lot, and this is where we spend the night. Although free camping is actually prohibited in Greece, it tends to be tolerated out of season.

Freestanding spot at the lagoon
Large parking lot at the lagoon, with a restaurant nearby
38°01'56.5" N, 22°52'23.8" E

Above: Details of the ruined city of Mystras
Below: Impressive structures in Delphi

We first drive to Nafplio and Tolo in the Peloponnese, neither of which really appealed to us, so we quickly continue to Mystras. We wind our way through what is now a ruined city, once containing forty thousand inhabitants. The metropolis is well preserved and fascinates us with its many beautiful details. The grounds are far reaching, and the upper city can even be visited through a second entrance that also has parking in front of it.

After the visit, we drive about an hour further, allowing us to eat breakfast directly on the beach the next morning. Our camper sits a few yards behind us at the beautiful, modern Camping Gythion Bay, where we stay for two nights.

Camping Gythion Bay
Mavrovouni Beach, Gythion
Phone: +30 27330 225 22,
contact@gythiocamping.gr
Open from April 1 to October 31
36°43′46.2″ N, 22°32′43.0″ E

Actually, Monemvasia is not on our way, but for this spot we gladly invest the extra miles. Monemvasia is a small village on an island that is connected to the mainland by a bridge. The car-free village is nestled beautifully on a rock in the middle of the turquoise-colored ocean. Many small shops line the narrow streets to the large square in front of the church—after which it is much quieter, and the well-kept homes are snuggled tightly together. In one of the restaurants, we eat on the terrace, with a beautiful view midday, and enjoy the beautiful day.

For Easter, we chose a place with a unique tradition. We drive to Leonidio, check in at Camping Semeli, and enjoy a day at the beach. During the night from Saturday to Easter Sunday, the spectacle begins at 11 p.m. The large numbers of people are busy in the squares starting their sky lanterns. For this, a piece of fabric is dipped in gas or oil, attached to the bottom of the lantern, and lit, and after a few seconds the thin tissue paper construction lifts to the sky. On this night, hundreds of lanterns go up and light up the sky. This tradition is also accompanied by deafening fireworks, which, of course, are also lit by all the people. It's loud, and it stinks of sulfur and soot, but it is beautiful how the sky is lit. We will always remember this Easter night.

Above: View of the Corinth Canal
Below: Graffiti in the streets of Athens in the Exarchia neighborhood

Restaurant: The Tavern of Matoulas
Monemvasia
Phone: +30 27320 616 60, www.matoula.gr
36°41'13.5" N, 23°03'18.9" E

After this unique experience, it's time to leave the Peloponnese. We drive to Athens. There we park our campervan at Camping Athens and take the bus to the middle of the city.

Camping Semeli
Epar. Od. Astrous, Leonidio
Phone: +30 27570 229 95, info@camping-se-meli.gr
Open from April 1 to November 30
37°08'58.6" N, 22°53'31.3" E

Camping Athens
Leof. Athinon 198–200, Athens
Phone: +30 2105 81 41 14,
info@campingathens.com.gr
Open all year
38°00'31.5" N, 23°40'19.6" E

Museums tend not to be our thing, and we have already visited so many city ruins in Greece, so we decide to find more-specific places to visit. So, we climb Filopappou Hill and view the Acropolis from here—in the other direction we also can see to the port city of Piraeus. On Areopagus Hill we watch the sunset.

We are even closer to the Acropolis here and, at the same time, can watch the sunset behind Athens. We continue to Monastiraki on foot—the "in" neighborhood of the city. There are many bars here in the evening— during the day, the alleys become real shopping districts. We find street art in the Exarchia neighborhood, where almost every building is covered in graffiti. Among them are some true works of art. As we approach Hadrian's Gate, we are amazed because we can see the Olympieion—better known as the Temple of Olympian Zeus—and the Acropolis from here. When we also meet a wild Greek tortoise in the National Garden, a large park in the middle of the city, we are quite sure that Athens is one of the most exciting and diverse cities in the world.

At the end of our trip in Greece, we fit in a stop on the Pelion Peninsula. We spend multiple nights at Camping Sikia, which is beautifully situated over several terraces directly on the sea.

One day, we make a trip to Milies, where we hike along the rails of the narrow-gauge railroad back to Kala Nera. The train doesn't run very often—in addition, the steam engine is loud and very slow. We can witness this ourselves because after the first few miles, it actually did chug by. We still had enough time to position our cameras before the train passed. It is a beautiful hike with many picturesque views over the hills to the Pagasitikos Gulf. In the end, we take a shortcut through the olive grove and treat ourselves to a dip in the ocean.

We have been in Greece for around a month now. A really beautiful country with an unbelievable number of things to see. But now we want to continue—there are many countries in Europe still waiting for us.

Camping Sikia
Kato Gatzea, Volos
Phone: +30 24230 222 79,
info@camping-sikia.gr
Open all year
39°18'36.6" N, 23°06'35.1" E

Previous double page: View to the Acropolis from Filopappou Hill
Top left: Typical lunch in Greece—gyros/pita
Top right: Hike along the railroad tracks in Pelion
Below: Evening mood at Camping Sikia

comewithus2.com

SERBIA

0   15 mi.

Tetovo

SKOPJE

Matka Canyon

Mt. Korab
9,068 ft.

Vardar

*Jakupica range
8,333 ft.*

Veles

Kičevo

Prilep

Cerna

Camping
Rino 2

Ohrid

*Lake
Ohrid*

*Baba Mtn.
8,530 ft.*

Bitola

Sveti Naum

*Lake
Prespa*

● *E65*

Start and Finish
From Lake Ohrid to Skopje

Distance
241 miles (388 km)

Travel Time
± 6 hours, 35 minutes

Highlights
Lake Ohrid with Sveti Naum
Matka Canyon

North Macedonia

AROUND LAKE OHRID
AND THROUGH MATKA CANYON TO SKOPJE

"Riots in Skopje Parliament" is the headline that is spreading through Western media like wildfire, and we are standing at the border to Macedonia, or, as it is called today, "North Macedonia." We discuss at length what we should do, and decide to enter. We want to hear for ourselves, within the country, how the situation really is, and we first drive to Lake Ohrid. The reception at Camping Rino is fit for royalty. Our engine has barely stopped in our campervan, and a coffee and a homemade *raki* (schnapps) is already on the table. The campground owner is young and welcomes us warmly. A colorful mix of nationalities meet here.

Camping Rino
Struga, Kalishta
Phone: +389 70 87 82 56,
campingrino@gmail.com
Open all year
41°09′21.2″ N, 20°39′02.5″ E

Lake Ohrid is regarded as one of the oldest lakes in the world and was deemed a UNESCO World Heritage Site in 1979. That's reason enough to explore its banks a little closer. The city of the same name, Ohrid, is a place of contrasts. Narrow streets with small shops, but also large, modern hotel compounds. We feel that tourism is nothing foreign here, but it does not feel overrun. Many captains offer their ships for excursions at the harbor—behind them, a few people enjoy their day with a coffee on the boardwalk. Our discovery tour continues along the lake, past the Bay of Bones. This village built on stilts on the lake is also an open-air museum.

Our actual goal, however, is Sveti Naum, a monastery about 19 miles (30 km) south of Ohrid and only a small leap away from the Albanian border. Saint Naum built the monastery and was also buried there. In the inner courtyard of the large compound is the monastery church, which has walls covered with many frescos.

Above: View of Lake Ohrid from Camping Rino
Below: Skopje with its magnificent city center

In the surrounding forest, there are also plenty of springs that can be reached either by foot or by boat.

Back at Camping Rino, we ask the owner and the many travelers from the north how the situation currently is in the capital. What we hear is unanimous—there is no problem! The conflict occurred only within Parliament. With that, there is nothing standing in the way of a visit to Skopje, and we drive to the capital. About 6 miles (10 km) from the center of Skopje, there is a campground near Hotel Bellevue. Compared to Camping Rino, it is twice as expensive, and the sanitary facilities are less clean. There are no alternatives. The campground itself is in a nice location, with even parking spots and large trees.

Camping Hotel Bellevue
Street 32 24, Ilinden
Phone: +389 2257 38 80,
bellevue-skopje@bestwestern-ce.com
Open all year
41°59'47.9" N, 21°33'00.4" E

We travel to the city center by public bus, and we are already struck after just a few yards. No, not literally—the location is absolutely calm—rather, it's the massive, grandiose structures such as we have not seen at all driving through the country thus far. Giant palaces and bridges, massive statues, and everything richly covered with gold. To us, this new architecture, designed to look old, just seems ostentatious. We like the old bazaar and the walk on the fortress wall of Kale, with a view down to Skopje, much better. Even when asking locals, we are commonly told that there aren't many things to see in North Macedonia, but we did get one tip: Matka Canyon! The canyon lies about 9 miles (15 km) southwest of Skopje, a true natural paradise. At Glumovo we exit the highway A2/E-65 and follow the signs. At the entrance to the canyon, we must decide if we want to explore the canyon on foot, by boat, or in a canoe. We decide to hike along the steep slopes and get continuously beautiful views of the river and the nature here. A place really worth visiting.

Despite our beginning skepticism, stirred up through Western media, our stay in North Macedonia was a really terrific experience. We once again encountered the typical hospitality of the Balkans and were able to explore super-beautiful landscapes.

Top left: A homemade, delicious corn pizza at Camping Rino
Top right: Warm welcome with coffee and schnapps at Camping Rino
Below: The Matka Canyon can be explored by foot or by boat.

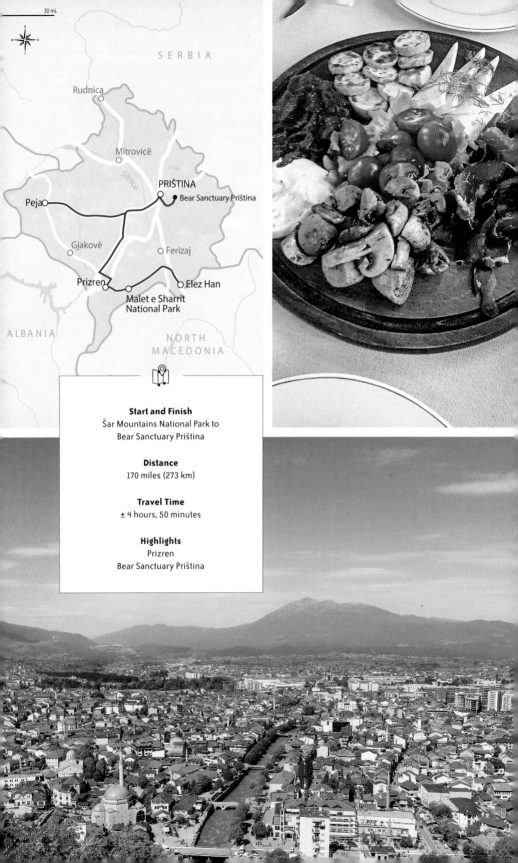

SERBIA

Rudnica

Mitrovicë

Sitnica

PRIŠTINA
● Bear Sanctuary Priština

Peja

Gjakovë

Ferizaj

Prizren

Elez Han

Malet e Sharrit
National Park

ALBANIA

NORTH
MACEDONIA

30 mi.

Start and Finish
Šar Mountains National Park to
Bear Sanctuary Priština

Distance
170 miles (273 km)

Travel Time
± 4 hours, 50 minutes

Highlights
Prizren
Bear Sanctuary Priština

THROUGH THE MOUNTAINS TO PRIZREN
AND TO THE BEAR SANCTUARY BEHIND PRIŠTINA

Restaurant Vila Park
Road Prizren, Brezovica on 12th km, Sredska
Phone: +377 44 295 973, vilapark@live.com
42°10'15.8" N, 20°50'46.4" E

Kosovo is the youngest country in Europe—it was only in 2008 when the country declared its independence from Serbia, which to this day does not recognize this decision. Travel into the country is somewhat more difficult: we must have liability insurance for our campervan at the border, which costs us fifteen euros for fifteen days. The customs control itself is done quickly, however.

First, we travel through the Šar Mountains National Park in Kosovo in the south of the country. A lot of green dominates this region of the Šar Planina mountain range, with mountain peaks at 8,858 feet (2,700 m) above sea level. At a restaurant directly on the R115, we finally ask if we can spend the night in the parking lot, since there are no campgrounds in all of Kosovo. "Of course, no problem," the owner tells us—we are able to speak in German. We eat dinner in the restaurant and especially enjoy the platter with the regional dishes.

We arrive in Prizren the next day well rested. We are walking through the alleys when we are approached: "Hello, where are you from? *Ah, Schwizerland Grüezi Grüezi!*" (Swiss German for "Switzerland, hello, hello!"). It turns out that the friendly man worked in Switzerland for a long time. He gives us many tips about what we should look at in the city, and invites us to park our campervan in his yard. He would gladly provide us with water and electricity. Unfortunately, the access road is too narrow, so we are not able to accept his offer. We take a walk—this time with a defined goal—and climb up the 1,722-foot hill (525 m) to reach Kalaja Fortress. The view of Prizren is terrific—we like the Ottoman-style city very much.

Above: Platter with regional delicacies in Restaurant Vila Park
Below: View over Prizren from Kalaja Fortress

Back in the city center, we visit the cathedral and the Sinan Pasha Mosque and make our way along the Prizren Bistrica river back to our van. On the road in Kosovo, we constantly encounter KFOR (Kosovo Force) troops, who are sent from different countries. To this day, they provide peace and security in the country. However, it is a sight to get used to.

In Priština, the traffic chaos catches up with us. Everyone drives the way they want, and because Friday mass has ended precisely at this moment, thousands of people are out on the roads, either on foot or in vehicles. It is impossible to find a parking spot. We only want to get out of the city. So, we continue directly to our next destination: the bear sanctuary, a FOUR PAWS project. Here, bears that were previously in private holdings or held in small cages in front of restaurants find a humane place to live, with an educational component for the public.

On the way to Peja, which is home to the best-tasting beer in Europe according to Lui, we sleep in a hotel. In these locations, it is simply easier to book a room than to find a quiet parking spot for the night. We drive through the Bjeshkët e Nemuna National Park as we make our way to Montenegro.

The difficult situation with accommodations is finally what makes us leave the small country, roughly a quarter of the size of Switzerland, after only two nights. An interesting country, with lots of nature, that will definitely be interesting for camping travelers as well in a few years.

Priština Bear Sanctuary
On the M25-2 to Mramor, then follow the northern bank of the lake to the west until arriving at the bear sanctuary (marked)
Phone: +383 44 609 044,
www.bearsanctuary-prishtina.org
April–October: 10:00 a.m.–7:00 p.m.
November–March: 10:00 a.m.–4:00 p.m.
42°38'11.3" N, 21°15'28.8" E

Above: The Prizrenscka Bistrica river flows through the middle of the city of Prizren.
Below: Steffi in the Priština Bear Sanctuary

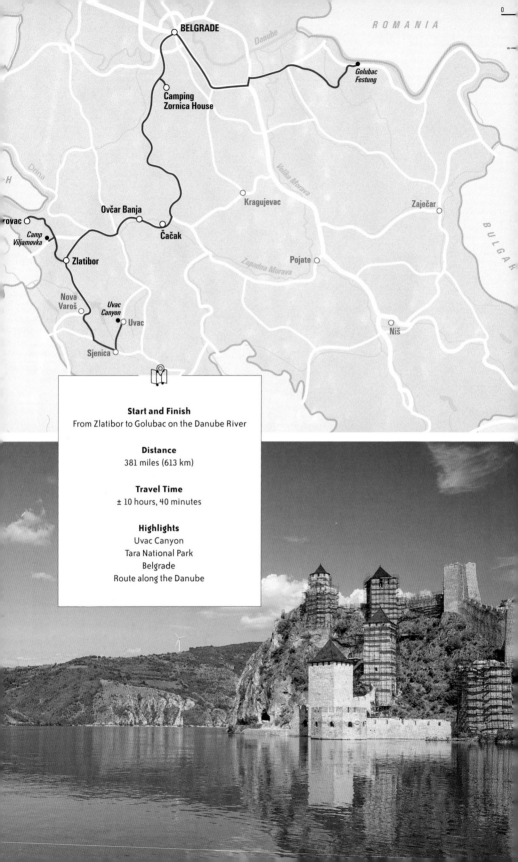

ROMANIA

BELGRADE

Golubac
Festung

Camping
Zornica House

Danube

Velika Morava

Kragujevac

Zaječar

Ovčar Banja

rovac

Camp
Viljamovka

Čačak

BULGAR

Zlatibor

Pojate

Zapadna Morava

Drina

Nova
Varoš

Uvac
Canyon

Uvac

Niš

Sjenica

Start and Finish
From Zlatibor to Golubac on the Danube River

Distance
381 miles (613 km)

Travel Time
± 10 hours, 40 minutes

Highlights
Uvac Canyon
Tara National Park
Belgrade
Route along the Danube

Serbia

UNDISCOVERED BEAUTIES IN THE BALKANS: UVAC, TARA NATIONAL PARK, OVČAR KABLAR

An entry directly from Kosovo is possible only if you already traveled into Kosovo via Serbia, but we came from North Macedonia, so we had to make a little detour through Montenegro in order to enter Serbia easily.

In Zlatibor, we check in to Kamp Zlatibor. This is also where the mandatory registration with the police takes place within twenty-four hours of arrival. Starting now, according to the manager, the registration is completed, and even if we spent a night in a freestanding spot, it wouldn't be a problem. And that's how it was . . .

We want to explore the river bends of the Uvac Canyon. This goal ends up not being so easy, because no one can speak English in the visitor center in Nova Varos. But we are warmly welcomed, and they quickly find someone in the telephone book who can explain everything to us. It isn't going to be possible with our camper, so we book a local guide and hop in Moloje-Mika's SUV a little later. A few steep meadow slopes, deep muddy ruts, and potholes later, and we have arrived at the Vidikovac Viewpoint and enjoy the terrific views. At the end, we drink a beer with our guide's brother in Restaurant Uvac.

Kamp Zlatibor
E-763, Zlatibor
Phone: +381 31 84 51 03, camp@zlatibor.org.rs
Open from April 1 to October 1
43°43'17.0" N, 19°42'31.0" E

Hike Uvac Canyon
Start at Restaurant Uvac (43°20'12.3" N, 19°59'15.7" E)
Follow the hiking trail to the Vidikovac Viewpoint. About 3 miles (5 km) / 1:15 hours each way (the way back is the same).
4x4 parking directly at Restaurant Uvac is possible (overnight stay possible), without 4x4 on the first hill after the beginning of the gravel road at the latest (plus approx. 1 mile (1.6 km) / 25 min. each way).

Golubac Fortress on the Danube River—Romania is on the other bank of the river.

Today we want to hike in Tara National Park. A good starting point is the visitor's center in Mitrovac. We get information in English about the different hikes and buy ourselves a detailed hiking map. Along the route, everything is very professionally marked—are we in a different country? We decide to follow Route 9, which should take us to the Banjska Stena viewpoint. The 7.6 miles (12.2 km) and 1,000 feet (305 m) in altitude should be doable in three hours and fifty-five minutes, according to the map. The forest becomes increasingly dense, with the path turning into a beaten track toward the end—and then we get our first views, followed by further ones. Wow, it's beautiful, and thanks to the map we also know right away that we are looking at the Drina River, which divides Serbia from Bosnia and Herzegovina with its flowing water.

In the campground guide of Serbia—written in German, of course—we find Viljamovka Camping. The elderly owner welcomes us with a homemade schnapps, and even without a common language we understand that it is made from the pears that grow here, in the distillery located directly next to the open-air reception.

Between Ovčar Banja and Čačak, there are not only many different trails, but also a total of ten monasteries that can be visited. We decided on Blagoveštenje Monastery, which had a well-maintained garden and an accessible bell tower that we enjoyed.

Farther on the way to Belgrade, we spend the night at Camping Zornica House, which is located not very far from the E-763. A small oasis of quiet, surrounded only by the many farm animals.

We take a whole day for the capital city. We park our camper near Belgrade Fortress and explore it, including its associated Kalemegdan Park. From the fortress walls, you have the best view of the merging of the Sava and the Danube.

Camping Zornica House
Zivorada Jankovica 13, Baćevac
Phone: +381 69 254 02 54,
recepcija@zornicakuca.rs
Open all year, except for Mondays and Tuesdays; please register for those days
43°50′42.3″ N, 19°34′27.3″ E

Mini-Kamping Viljamovka
Selo Kremna, Mokra Gora
Phone: +381 63 842 98 08,
camping.viljamovka@gmail.com
Open from May 1 to October 1
43°50′42.3″ N, 19°34′27.3″ E

Above: Our parking spot at Mini-Kamping Viljamovka
Below: View from the Vidikovac Viewpoint of the Uvac

Knez Mihailova Street is regarded as the shopping street and pedestrian area in Belgrade and leads past Republic Square, which next to its different monuments and museums is regarded as *the* location for Serbian tourism. At Zeleni Venac—a year-round farmers' market—we fall once again for the *burek* (filled pastry). On the way back, we walk through the Stari Grad (old city) and arrive in the Skadarlija district, where we need to have a bite to eat in at least one of the famous three pubs—Tri Šešira (Three Hats), Dva Jelena (Two Deer), and Šešir Moj (My Hat).

Following the Danube, we leave Belgrade, and after a stop at Golubac Fortress—the entrance to the Iron Gate gorge where the Danube forms the border with Romania—we leave the country. From the well-marked routes in Tara National Park to the hidden gems at Uvac Canyon—anyone can find exactly what they want here, and much more.

Restaurant Tri Šešira
Skadarska 29, Belgrade
Phone: +381 60 313 01 80
Open daily from 11:00 a.m. to midnight
44°49′04.2″ N, 20°27′51.2″ E
Dva Jelena and Šešir Moj are located right next to it (open daily from 10:00 a.m. to 1:00 a.m.).

Entrance to Kalemegdan Park in Belgrade

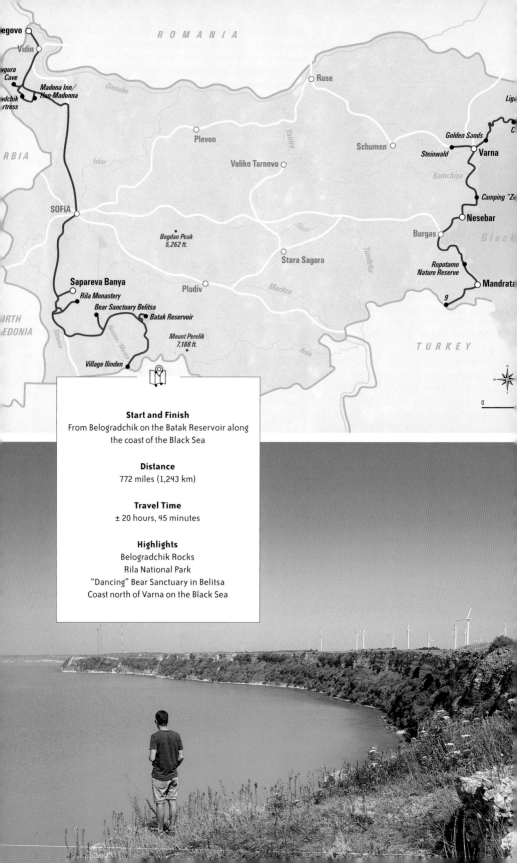

R O M A N I A

egovo

Vidin

agura
Cave

Madona Inn/
Han-Madonna

adchik
rtress

RBIA

Danube

Ruse

Lig

Pleven

Schumen

Golden Sands

Steinwald

Varna

C

RTH
EDONIA

Iskar

SOFIA

Bogdan Peak
5,262 ft.

Veliko Tarnovo

Yantra

Kamchiya

Camping "Ze

Nesebar

Stara Sagora

Burgas

Black

Sapareva Banya

Rila Monastery

Bear Sanctuary Belitsa

Batak Reservoir

Plodiv

Struma

Mesta-Nestos

Mount Perelik
7,188 ft.

Village Ilinden

Maritza

Tundzha

Ropotamo
Nature Reserve

Mandrata

9

Arda

T U R K E Y

0

Start and Finish
From Belogradchik on the Batak Reservoir along
the coast of the Black Sea

Distance
772 miles (1,243 km)

Travel Time
± 20 hours, 45 minutes

Highlights
Belogradchik Rocks
Rila National Park
"Dancing" Bear Sanctuary in Belitsa
Coast north of Varna on the Black Sea

Bulgaria

SURPRISING LANDSCAPES NEAR BELOGRADCHIK AND IN RILA NATIONAL PARK

Even before arriving at border control, we are already stopped: Buy vignette here! The tolls in Bulgaria are not only for interstates, but also for individual highways. Good, we can buy the monthly vignette for fifteen euros directly at the customs point. Now it's time to go—into our twelfth country.

The main roads are new and in good condition thanks to the EU. As we turn off the E79 toward Belogradchik, the nice roads come to an end. Before we explore the region over the next few days, we first park our van at Camping Han Madona and eat regional specialties in the accompanying restaurant.

Camping Han Madona
Madona Inn Falkovets, Road 114, Yanyovets
Phone: +359 894 77 47 46,
info@hanmadona.com
Open all year
43°35'52.4" N, 22°46'47.6" E

A unique landscape stretches from Rabisha to Belotintsi, and our destination of Belogradchik is directly in the middle. During our approach, we already marvel at the giant rocks made of sandstone, which stretch far above the treetops. We use the parking bays and catch grand views of the landscape. In Belogradchik itself, a castle is built within one of these giant rocks, which we explore as well. Magura Cave, which is known for its cave drawings, is located not very far from here. We explore the caves wearing thick sweaters and repeatedly end up disturbing bats—a truly exciting attraction.

We leave out Sofia, the capital city, and drive directly to Rila National Park. Here we view the Rila Monastery, an especially beautiful building with countless murals. In this region there is even more to see: for example, the Stob Earth Pyramids, which are bizarre rock formations, with some even having natural stone hats. On the way to Camping Verila in Saparewa Banja, we even pass the famous geyser.

The northern coast of Bulgaria south of Cape Kaliakra

Unfortunately, the geyser was forced into a water fountain construction, which led us to not find it particularly appealing.

Camping Verila
Sapareva Banya
Phone: +359 88 884 37 59, tsverila@abv.bg
Open all year
42°17′29.7″ N, 23°15′04.7″ E

We actually came to Rila National Park in order to hike around the Seven Rila Lakes. The chair lift, which should have brought us to the high plains, is not in operation this weekend because of the bad weather, and during the week it currently doesn't run at all. As a result, we must continue without seeing this highlight. About 93 miles (150 km) and a dirt road later, and we arrived at the bear sanctuary in Belitsa. A place of sorrow. The bears that live here have experienced only suffering and agony until being "freed" by the FOUR PAWS organization by being forced to dance chained up on the street and learning to do it on two legs by having to stand on burning coals.

"Dancing" Bear Sanctuary in Belitsa
Adrianov Chark, Belitsa
Phone: +359 88 244 13 77
Open from April 1 to October 31
42°01′47.0″ N, 23°34′36.4″ E

Less than two hours later, we check into Eco Camping Batak, a terrific spot on the banks of the Batak Reservoir. Due to a problem with our battery charger, our stay was involuntarily extended. But really, there are much-worse things than being stranded in a terrific camping spot with nice owners in the midst of beautiful nature. As soon as we replace the device a few days later, we want to continue on right away. So, we drive to Turkey through Greece. We will describe this route in the next chapter, but here we will jump directly to the Bulgarian coast along the Black Sea, which we drove after visiting Turkey.

At a maximum speed of 25 miles per hour (40 km/h), we make our way along Road 99 from the Turkish border to the Black Sea. Somewhat north of Primorsko we are rewarded with a sand dune and terrific views of the Ropotamo river delta. We hike through the natural conservation area along the coast and enjoy a few wonderful days here on the water, which, by the way, isn't black at all but shines in a beautiful turquoise color. Here on the southern coast of the Black Sea we find very run-down campgrounds, which win any points only because of their terrific location.

Inner courtyard of the beautiful Rila Monastery in the national park of the same name
Following double page: The spectacular columns in the rock forest at Dewnja

In the old city of Nessebar we encounter many Western tourists, many sporting all-inclusive armbands of diverse colors around their wrists. That quickly becomes too much tourism for us and too-little Bulgaria. So, we continue on and are soon sitting at the really beautiful Camping Zora in the middle of two Dutch travel groups with a total of thirty campers. We were lucky to find even a mini-spot here. All the tourists are leaving tomorrow, though, and then the campground will belong almost all to us.

Camping Zora
Treti mart Str. 66, Obzor
Phone: +359 89 821 80 27, www.zora-ob.com
Open from May 24 to October 15
42°49'28.0" N, 27°52'46.8" E

One of our YouTube viewers of our travels writes to us and tells us that she'd like to show us her favorite spots in Varna, which is also where she lives. Of course, we accept and, after a piece of homemade cake, explore the beach in Galata together with Margarita. It is a beautiful and lesser-known beach south of Varna, which is accessible over five hundred stairs. A small fishing village is located somewhat north of here, which we walk through, and the men there exchange a few words with our hostess.

We continue in the camper to the observation deck, where we can catch a view over all of Varna, including the harbor. The next destination is located about thirty minutes away in the backcountry: we want to go to the rock forest of Dwenja.

After we arrive, the woman selling tickets tells us that there aren't any parking attendants in the back parking lot today, and that it would be better if we parked our car on the street. We take such safety information seriously, of course, and first repark our campervan. Only then do we begin to explore this whimsical landscape. Pobiti Kamani, the actual name of the rock forest, can be translated as "rocks rammed into the ground." For a long time, it was widely accepted that the columns were remnants from Roman times, but today it has been proven that the columns emerged millions of years ago from the bottom of the sea.

In the late afternoon, we say goodbye to Margarita and let the day come to an end at Camping Laguna, north of Varna. Located on a slope, the spot is pretty nice, even if the warm water is off due to some sort of problem.

Camping Laguna
Varna
Phone: +359 89 860 04 03,
laguna@lagunavillageresort.com
Open from March 1 to October 31
43°18′23.8″ N, 28°03′11.3″ E

We spend our last day in Bulgaria far north along the coast. Margarita gave us a few tips yesterday on spots worth visiting in the north. Near Kavarna, we exit the E87 for the 901. We stubbornly follow this road until we arrive at Cape Kaliakra with its fortress. With cliffs around 230 feet (70 m) high, the view of the steep coast is spectacular. After more-careful observation, we could even see a porpoise and her calf. Yes, it's true—we really do like it here in the north.

To get to Bolata Beach, we must drive back a little and take the first small street to the right. We follow it to the beach and find a nice bay with a sandy beach at the foot of the cliffs.

The drive goes back to the 901 road, which we follow to Shabla Lighthouse. Along the way, we see a few old oil-pump stations, but the black gold hasn't streamed here in a long time. Much more interesting is the lighthouse, which still is a marker for seamen today, which they have made their way halfway along the route from the Bosporus Strait in Istanbul to the Danube Delta in Romania. We take this route as well, but on land. Now, we are about to put the first part of the route behind us and start the second by traveling through Romania. But in this book, we are first going to go to Turkey.

Above: A resident of the Bear Sanctuary in Belitsa—today he lives there in peace.
Below: Camping Kiten on the southern coast of Bulgaria—but appearances are deceiving.

BULGARIA

0   50 mi.

Edirne

İpsala   Istanbul   Izmit

Marmara-
meer

Çanakkale Destani
Museum   Bandırma

Hotel Kum   Çanakkale
Çanakkale   Bursa

Troy

Burhaniye

Izmir

Sea   Antalya

Start and Finish
From İpsala to Edirne

Distance
618 miles (995 km)

Travel Time
± 13 hours

Highlights
Çanakkale Destani Museum
Burhaniye
Istanbul

Turkey

GALLIPOLI PENINSULA,
BEACH LIFE IN BURHANIYE, AND ISTANBUL

Coming from Greece, we cross the border near İpsala. Our papers keep getting checked at multiple locations, and then we are finally in. Near Keşan, we turn onto the E87 to the south and find ourselves on the Gallipoli Peninsula soon after. The roads are good—most of them continue straight ahead endlessly. The nature along the highway isn't exactly lively: it is the beginning of July, and the sun is burning relentlessly in the sky.

The campground at Hotel Kum is recommended as a good spot to spend the night. So, we drive on the E87 until shortly before Eceabat and cross the peninsula. Unfortunately, the recommendation isn't exactly the best here; quite the opposite. The reception was, well, unique, but we didn't want to jump to any negative conclusions on our first day in the country—maybe it's just the culture here? The camping spots are between trees, and the electrical boxes probably date back to World War I. The sanitary facilities likely date back to the same era as well, including the

interior finishing. Simply put: old, broken, uncared for, and dirty. But the beach is worth visiting, so we lie down there and enjoy the terrific weather.

On the second day, we want to learn about the history of the Gallipoli Peninsula, so we drive to the Çanakkale Destanı War Museum, even though we aren't really museumgoers. We must have gone through some sort of time travel in the stairwell, because we arrived in the middle of the war in 1915. Different scenes are re-created with life-sized soldiers, tactics are discussed, and equipment and clothing are shown. All explanations are available in English. The absolute highlight is the 5-D cinema tour. Next to huge screens all around and on the ceiling, you go from room to room and even find yourself on a mining vessel at some point and feel the detonation—at another point you must make your way to the next room through a trench. You really feel like a part of the whole thing.

Above: Typical dinner in Turkey
Below: Our view at the campground in Altin

The only negative: the Turkish propaganda at the end is very exaggerated and really makes us aware of where we are again.

We want to continue to Çanakkale in our campervan and have picked out Eceabat as our ferry harbor. We get the tickets on-site and paid 27.50 Turkish lira (about six euros) for a one-way ticket for the two of us and our 16-foot (5 m) camper. The crossing of the Dardanelles took about thirty minutes, and we are already in Asia!

Following the E87 further, we pass by Troy and park the van in the visitor lot. As we see the entrance prices and the masses of people on the grounds, we decide that the view from this side of the fence is enough, and we continue. The destination for today is Camping Altin, near Burhaniye. After arriving, we park our camper directly on the water and decide to take a week off here.

After a few nights, we get German neighbors who have been coming to this site for the last thirty-five years during their trips to Turkey. We explore the surroundings with them, visit the Ören Tarihi Köy Pazarı vegetable market, and go to *kahvaltı* (brunch) in Nil's Garden on Sunday. We will never forget this breakfast as long as we live—it was heaven on Earth!

In general, the food in Turkey is just to our taste, and we end up sitting—even during the fasting month of Ramadan—in a different restaurant every day and eat like kings. Kebab platters, pitas, or Turkish pizzas: everything is fresh and delicious.

Restaurant Nil's Garden
Taylıeli Mahallesi, Burhaniye
Phone: +90 533 513 59 98
Open daily—reserve Sunday brunch (called kahvaltı)!
39°28'31.8" N, 26°55'52.3" E

Altin Camp & Park Hotel
Altinyol, Kurtdereli Caddesi No. 13, Burhaniye
Phone: +90 266 416 37 37, info@altincamp.com
Open from April 1 to October 31
39°30'37.8" N, 26°56'04.9" E

Ören Salonu Stand at the Market in Ören Mahallesi
Taylıeli Mahallesi, Burhaniye
39°30'02.6" N, 26°56'01.5" E

Restaurant Burhaniye Sofrasi
Mahkeme Mahallesi, Hürriyet Cd. Number 72, Burhaniye
39°30'06.9" N, 26°58'38.5" E

Above: Short ferry ride from Eceabat to Çanakkale
Below: The Trojan horse in Troy—but seen only through the fence

After a little more than a week, we can finally pull ourselves away and drive north. In Bandirma, we board another ferry, which brings us directly to Istanbul over the Sea of Marmara in about two and a half hours for approximately seventy Euros. We buy the ticket directly at the terminal.

Freestanding spot near Ahirkapi Park with twenty-four-hour parking attendants
Otopark, Sultan Ahmet Mahallesi,
Fatih/Istanbul
Parking possible day and night
41°00'05.8" N, 28°58'38.8" E

There is no campground in Istanbul itself, but a well-known open lot. We park our camper there around midday and go to the city center by foot. It is still Ramadan, so it is relatively quiet in the center.

Oh, there is so much to see in Istanbul! The Blue Mosque, the small and large Hagia Sophia, the Citadel, the Egyptian Bazaar, Gülhane Park, Galata Bridge, the restaurant boats under it—but the absolute highlight for us are the dolphins in the Bosporus Strait, which we can watch from the banks while they are hunting.

There are two opinions on night sleeping in the open lot. Steffi says, "Great spot, central location, and I slept great!" Lui, on the other hand, says, "Super-central location, but the police break up dealers at night in this parking lot. I didn't sleep at all." One night was enough for Lui, and the next afternoon we continued back to Bulgaria.

Above: The Hagia Sophia—one of the landmarks of Istanbul
Below: Evening mood at Camping Altin

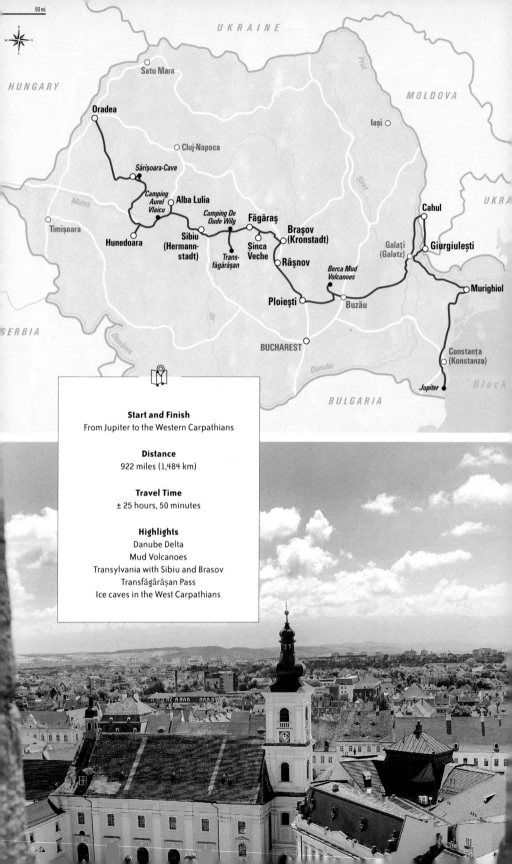

50 mi.

UKRAINE

HUNGARY

MOLDOVA

Satu Mare

Oradea

Iași

Cluj-Napoca

Sărișoara-Cave

Camping
Aurel
Vlaicu

Alba Lulia

Camping De
Oude Wilg

Făgăraș

Cahul

Mureș

UKRA

Timișoara

Hunedoara

Sibiu
(Hermann-
stadt)

Trans-
făgărășan

Sinca
Veche

Brașov
(Kronstadt)

Galați
(Galatz)

Giurgiulești

Râșnov

Berca Mud
Volcanoes

Murighiol

SERBIA

Ploiești

Buzău

BUCHAREST

Constanța
(Konstanza)

Danube

Jupiter

Black

BULGARIA

Start and Finish
From Jupiter to the Western Carpathians

Distance
922 miles (1,484 km)

Travel Time
± 25 hours, 50 minutes

Highlights
Danube Delta
Mud Volcanoes
Transylvania with Sibiu and Brasov
Transfăgărășan Pass
Ice caves in the West Carpathians

Romania and Moldova

FROM THE DANUBE DELTA THROUGH MOLDOVA TO MUD VOLCANOES, MOUNTAIN PASSES, AND UNIQUE CITIES

Actually, we had already picked out a terrific campground right across the Romanian border, but unfortunately we find out on-site that only tents are allowed. So, we drive through two villages respectively named 2 May and 23 August in order to finally reach Jupiter—okay, the local town names are really unusual! Camping Popas Zodiac also turns out to be a good choice; everything is clean and in good condition—we don't need much more.

Camping Popas Zodiac
Gala Galaction Nr. 49, Jupiter, Mangalia
Phone: +40 743 33 41 94,
papaszodiac@gmail.com
Open from April 15 to October 31
43°51′33.7″ N, 28°35′56.1″ E

The Romanian coast along the Black Sea really doesn't win us over. So, we decide to drive directly to the Danube delta and spend some more time there, where we like it much better.

After arriving in Murighiol, we decide to stay at Camping Lac Murighiol, where the owner explains to us during check-in that he also offers boat tours of the Danube delta. We book the three-hour tour right away for the next morning—it's supposed to start before sunrise.

Camping Lac Murighiol
Murighiol str Mahmudiei Nr. 10, Murighiol
Phone: +40 744 17 55 81,
contact@campinglacmurighiol.ro
Open from April 15 to October 15
45°02′27.7″ N, 29°09′22.8″ E

Along with the owner, we are the only ones in the small, six-person boat. First, we cross two large channels and then delve into the maze of the Danube delta. We fit everywhere in the small boat, pass through floating reed islands, and make our way even farther into the network of small channels. The time of day is perfect for watching birds.

View from above of Sibiu—Steffi made it to the top of the church tower.

We see cormorants, night herons, spoonbills, and much more, but great white pelicans were the most special, warming themselves in the morning sun. Yes, we will remember this day for a very long time to come.

Actually, we felt at the time that we would like to go to Odessa in Ukraine, which would have been possible in 2018. So, the next day, we decide to attempt to travel there through Moldova. We can't find any campgrounds in our research, and we aren't quite pioneering enough to park in the open for multiple days ... but nevertheless, we leave in the early morning and find ourselves at the border crossing from Romania into Moldova near Galați in the late morning, but we are stuck there for over five hours in the blazing heat. Okay, our plan has a weak spot ... We have to forget about Ukraine for the time being—we need a solution in Moldova, so we drive north into the country. Two policemen wave us over, but when Lui rolls down the window he is met with the smell of alcohol. No, not drunken policemen, on top of everything else! Since we don't speak any common language, they let us keep driving right away. The roads are extremely bad, so we must drive at a speed of about 25 miles per hour (40 km/h) in temperatures of over 85°F (30°C). It becomes clear to us that our progress is coming to a standstill. We are really feeling down in the dumps, and the problems at the border and the drunk policemen really rubbed us the wrong way, so we decide to drive back to Romania today. According to our street atlas, the next border station should be near Cahul. After about an hour we pass through, a little later we are pulled over on the Romanian side by the police, and finally we book the first hotel we can find. Okay, Moldova was only a short detour, but at least it *was* one.

Restaurant La Hangar with camping area
DC108, Aleea Vulcanilor
Phone: +40 744 55 45 53
Open from April 1 to October 31
45°20'49.1" N, 26°42'35.4" E

We got the tip from other travelers to go to the mud volcanoes in Berca. And today we are back to being fully motivated. We get a little lost in the mini-streets, but we end up finding our destination. At the foot of the muddy landscape is a restaurant with a camping area. This is our starting point the next morning for the mud volcanoes. As the sun first starts to appear, we are alone and hear bubbling from the volcanoes all around us. There are countless small craters in this moonscape. It is really terrific here!

Above: The inner city of Sibiu is so wonderfully colorful—the houses as well as the flowers.
Below: In Moldova, the draw wells are still in operation in the villages.

After exploring the natural wonders, it's time to move to the cities. We drive to Transylvania and check into the Camping Cheile Râsnoavei in Râşnov for multiple days. We do a free walking tour in Braşov and can't believe our eyes: Wow, this city is beautiful! So colorful and full of life, and at the same time very clean with many small shops to attract customers. Unbelievable; we did not expect to find something like this in Romania! We have a similar experience in Râşnov. There is not as much activity here, but the view down from the castle ruins is spectacular.

Camping Cheile Râsnoavei
Strada Cheia, Râşnov
Phone +40 733 071 200
Open from May 1 to September 30
45°20'49.1" N, 26°42'35.4" E

We don't spend much time in Bran, not because we fear Dracula but because there are way too many tourists walking around, and the prices are at least twice as high compared to the towns before. The monastery Mănăstirea Rupestră Şinca Veche is much more in accord with our taste. Over seven thousand years ago, a temple was carved out of granite stone. A skylight illuminates a cross. Around it is a monastery with very well-kept grounds.

Cave Church & Şinca Veche Monastery
Parking lot, 45°45'20.9" N, 25°09'54.1" E

We follow highway 73A to the end and turn onto the E68 in order to reach Făgăraş, where we view the Făgăraş Citadel. An exhibit spanning numerous floors is available to view, and in it we make our way through the prison tower and the chambers of the nobles. If there's one thing you can count on, it's the Dutch. The Dutch-influenced campground Camping Oude Wilg is no exception: beautifully located among the greenery, it is simply a gem. We wait here for some better weather, because we want to get out again and would like some sunshine.

Moated Castle in Făgăraş
45°50'42.6" N, 24°58'28.0" E

Camping de Oude Wilg
Str. Prund 40, Carta
Phone: +40 269 52 13 47,
www.campingdeoudewilg.com
Open from March 1 to October 31
45°47'02.1" N, 24°34'01.7" E

Above: Evening meal in Braşov—of course with polenta as a side
Below: It's 95°F (35°C) aboveground, and below in the ice cave, towers of ice—marvelous!

This time we're lucky—the sun comes out a few days later, and we drive the Transfăgărășan Pass, using the road 7C heading from north to south. Because of the harsh winter, the pass road is navigable only from July to October. Good that we left ourselves so much time before—it's the beginning of July, so we can manage the hairpin curves in good conditions. We take advantage of the many stopping bays to get out and enjoy the views and nature. After a few more curves, we arrive at the top of the pass at a height of 6,699 feet (2,042 m) above sea level. It's cool up here, but we still take a nice walk along the Bâlea Lake.

There is a guesthouse at the lake, at which we warm up. Farther ahead along the street, there are a few market stands that sell regional specialties. We drive through the tunnel and a few hundred yards down the southern side, then we turn around because we still want to go to Sibiu, and that lies at the northern part of the pass.

Sibiu, or, as it's known in German, "Hermannstadt," impressed us at our first visit. The colorful houses, the lush flowers, the friendly people—and there's always a lot going on here. We decide to stay a few more days at Camping Ananas in Cisnădioara to explore Sibiu a little more thoroughly. We explore not only the city, but also the surrounding area; for example, we visit the Astra Open Air Museum and walk to the Cisnădioara ruins. Before we finally leave Sibiu, we buy a sticker for our campervan. Yes, this city has really done it to us.

We continue to Alba Iulia, one of the oldest settlements in Romania. Only from the air can you see its most unusual characteristic: the city walls form the shape of a star. We explore the old city from the ground and look at the many historical monuments and churches. We spend the night at Camping Aurel Vlaicu. The spot is unfortunately a bit grubby, but it's fine for one night.

Camping Ananas Sibiu
Strada Pinului, Cisnădioara
Phone: +40 741 74 66 89, info@ananas7b.de
Open from April 15 to October 20
45°42′25.7″ N, 24°06′19.2″ E

Camping Aurel Vlaicu
Aurel Vlaicu 335401, Romania
Phone: +40 254 245 541,
denniswiskerke@hotmail.com
Open from April 15 to October 15
45°42′25.7″ N, 24°06′19.2″ E

Above: Selfie with the residents of the Astra Open Air Museum
Below: View of the curves of the pass road of Transfăgărășan

Next stop is Hunedoara, known in English as Corvin Castle. In contrast to at Bran, a truly imposing castle stands here, which can also be visited. Because we are here on a Saturday, there is a lot going on, but we still want to see the castle from the inside and go over the narrow bridge to the main entrance. The building is huge—many twisted paths lead through the imposing castle, which has also been the backdrop for many films. For example, *Martin Luther* and *Nostradamus* were filmed here, and even Kelly Clarkson has filmed a music video here.

In the end, we treat ourselves to a chimney cake, a specialty baked over open coals, before we drive into the last remaining region in Romania—the West Carpathians. Erwin is already expecting us when we arrive. He lives here and offers travelers a spot in his huge yard. If you want to spend the night at Erwin's, you must register beforehand, which is how he knows that we are arriving.

Erwin gives us countless tips on what we can do in the West Carpathians. In Apuseni Natural Park, we take a hike to the Groapa Ruginoasa ravine. After the first few yards, we find a kiosk on the side of the path—fresh pancakes with jam made from the berries of the region are sold here! Some provisions for the journey wouldn't be a bad thing, so we take advantage of the opportunity.

Private, overnight spot at Erwin's
DN75 1, Arieşeni
Phone: +40 785 18 57 86, register at
www.westkarpaten.ro/anfrage/
Open all year only with registration
46°28'21.0" N, 22°45'40.9" E

And to finish, an absolute highlight: we visit the Scărişoara Ice Cave. It's almost 86°F (30°C) aboveground, but a couple of dozen steps down and the temperatures lie below freezing. The cave floor is completely covered by a thick layer of ice—naturally. Wow, we are excited, even if we can't understand a word the guide, who has a lot to explain to our group, says.

That was our last day in Romania. Wistfully, we let it come to an end with Erwin at the river. He brings us some pine cone syrup, and we review our four weeks spent in the country. What an absolutely wonderful country, with great infrastructure for campers. Romania will always be one of our top three countries, and we recommend visiting it to everyone, from the bottom of our hearts.

Above: On a birdwatching tour through the Danube delta—a night heron
Below: The market square in Braşov—this is where we really fell in love with Romania.

SLOVAKIA

Bükk
National
Park

Tokaj

Miskolc

Tisa

Kékes
3,330 ft.

Eger

STRIA

Lake
Neusiedl

Sopron

Danube

Győr

BUDAPEST

Hortobágy

Debrecen

Szombathely

Székesfehérvár

Lake Balaton

Kecskemét

ROMANI

Drava

Pécs

Szeged

Mureș

ROATIA

SERBIA

30 mi.

Start and Finish
From Debrecen to Győr

Distance
349 miles (561 km)

Travel Time
± 7 hours, 30 minutes

Highlights
Steppe in Hortobágy
Wine regions, including Tokaj and Eger
Budapest

Hungary

STEPPE, ENCHANTING WINE REGIONS, THERMAL BATHS, AND BUDAPEST

We need an e-vignette to pay the road tolls in Hungary. It's possible to get them online before entering, but since we wanted to stay spontaneous with our arrival time, we buy one in Romania shortly before crossing the border. For one month, we pay just under forty euros. What's important for the e-vignette are details such as checking the license plate number, the country of registration, and the correct vehicle category—campers are D2. Even one typo can cause big problems. For us, everything checks out, so our trip into Hungary starts off smoothly.

We make our first stop in Debrecen—at Camping Lyra Beach, we plan our route through Hungary and jump now and then into the pool. In the evening, we prefer the thermal pools.

Camping Lyra Beach Debrecen
Debrecen, Szávay Gyula u. 22
Phone: +36 30 477 49 75,
kempingdebrecen@gmail.com
www.kerekestelepifurdo.hu
Open all year
47°30'30.1" N, 21°38'16.6" E

We were often told that Hungary was going to be boring—probably because it's so flat. But flat can also be very interesting. That's why we drive to Hortobágy National Park. That's where we want to explore the Pustza—the steppe. And because Steffi is such a horse girl, she already knows that this trip can be wonderfully combined with a visit to the Máta Stud Farm in Mátai Ménes. We just missed the carriage ride. No worries; another will depart in about two hours, and in that time we can visit the stalls of the Nonius horses. And that's what we do for 120 minutes. Mares with foals, mares without foals, studs, and everything—including the cats—are petted.

Then our tour on the Puszta begins. We travel out on the carriage into the vastness, view the original stables, and are shown that longhorns not only are good looking but also can pull when harnessed to a cart, and, of course, we see more horses.

Discover Hungarian steppe cattle on the Puszta of Hortobágy.

Yes, we saw a whole equestrian show in the traditional riding style. Our horse girl is in seventh heaven, but Lui is not quite there yet.

Carriage ride starting at the Máta Stud Farm to the Hortobágy Nature Center
Hortobágy, Máta major 48
Phone +36 52 58 91 10, www.hortobagy.eu/hu/
Open all year
47°35′40.7″ N, 21°09′13.2″ E

It was when he finally discovered the outdoor and thermal pools at Camping Castrum Thermal that he was completely satisfied with the day. Another camping spot that includes a thermal pool! Yes, we like it very much.

The journey continues in the north. Tokaj is a small city with beautiful, colorful houses; good maintenance; and known beyond borders for its wine.

Hajdúböszörmény Castrum Thermalkemping
Hajdúböszörmény, Nagy András u. 26
Phone: +36 20 959 19 31,
info@bocskaitermal.hu
Open from April 1 to October 31
47°41′01.7″ N, 21°29′56.9″ E

Until now, we were familiar only with the sweet variety, but we learn on-site that there is also a dry version of this lovely wine, aszú. We also learn that the sweetness in Tokaji aszú comes from a portion of botrytized, shriveled grapes, which have a much-higher sugar content. It's only one of the many ways Tokaji gets its light-amber color.

We taste our way through the assortment and bring a bottle with us back to the camper. It's parked directly on the Tisza—the river—at Camping Mayfly.

The location is terrific, but the sanitary facilities are not. Right next to it is Restaurant Halra Bor Étterem, where we eat assorted meat dishes and drink even more regional wine.

interesting day come to an end over a glass of wine. Wine from Hungary—we won't ever let ourselves doubt it again.

Camping Mayfly
Rakamaz, Horgász u. 11/a
Phone: +36 70 934 41 76,
tiszaviragcamping@gmail.com
Open from April 1 to October 30
48°07′24.7″ N, 21°25′05.6″ E
Restaurant Halra Bor Étterem
48°07′20.7″ N, 21°25′0.08″ E

Tulipán Kemping
Eger, Tulipánkert u. 3
Phone: +36 70 385 11 66,
info@tulipancamping.com
Open from March 15 to October 15
47°53′38.2″ N, 20°21′32.2″ E

Valley of the Beautiful Women in Eger
Wine cellars in caves as bars with small bites
Eger, Almási Pál u. 38
47°53′25.2″ N, 20°21′32.2″ E

On the way to Eger, we pass Bükki National Park. In Lillafüred, we hike through the forest and look at the hanging gardens, including a waterfall. In Eger, we park the van at Camping Tulipán and go on foot into the Valley of the Beautiful Women—the name of the wine region in the town. It is a park with public grills surrounded by stone wine cellars, all of which offer wine to taste and bites to eat. We taste our way through the mostly white wines and are advised very competently in English. By the way, in Eger there are over two hundred of these wine cellars, but not all of them have been converted to bars as well. We let this

Before we devote ourselves to the capital city—it is currently too full due to a major event—we drive farther east—more specifically, to Győr. It is unbelievably hot today, which is why we walk into the center of the city at sunset. We have already discovered many people at Lakeside Camping Győr who are waiting for a dentist appointment. In the town itself we now see more dental practices than cafés! We shortly consider whether we should also make an appointment but ultimately decide against it. Dentists aren't really our thing.

Previous double page: One of the most famous wine towns in Hungary—Tokaj
Top left: Simple lunch at the Máta Stud Farm
Top right: Apéro and wine in the Valley of the Beautiful Women—in Eger
Below: Ruin pub Szimpla Kert in the Jewish quarter in Budapest

Once we ask, the manager at the campground explains to us that many foreigners come to this town to get dental work done for a low price: business is flourishing, and the prices are rising. This is still not a problem for the foreigners, but the locals haven't been able to afford to get dental work done here for a long time.

Tópart Camping Győr
Győr, Mákosdülőutca 7
Phone: +36 96 31 17 45,
topartcamping@freemail.hu
Open from April 15 to October 15
47°53'38.2" N, 20°21'32.2" E

In the end, we drive to the capital. We park our campervan not too far from the heart of the city, at Camping Arena Budapest, and take the train into the center. We learn quickly that Buda lies on one bank of the Danube, and Pest on the other. Over the course of history, the cities were put together and Budapest was born. Today it is one of the most visited European cities. Sure, it can't really compete with the charm of Eger or Tokaj, but there are some really exciting areas; for example, in the Jewish Quarter. Kazinczy Street is especially unique, and here we find many restaurants and special ruin pubs—which are bars in dilapidated buildings. We get ourselves a drink in the most famous one—Szimpla Kert. Right next to it is the Karaván Street Food Market, where we have a small bite to eat. The central market hall was unfortunately already closed, so we missed it, but instead we end up wandering on the Danube promenade right at sunset on the Pest side—this is also where the small bronze Little Princess statue sits. The many bridges and the Parliament building literally glow in the setting sun. We reach Castle Hill in the Buda district at night, but the buildings are beautifully illuminated, the temperature is comfortable, and the streets are still full of people. To finish off our discovery tour, we land at Fisherman's Bastion—where we enjoy a terrific view of Pest from its terraces.

Camping Arena Budapest
Budapest, Pilisi u. 7/a
Phone: +36 30 296 91 29,
info@budapestcamping.hu
Open all year
47°30'14.6" N, 19°09'28.2" E

And so, our travel in Hungary ends. If there was one thing we didn't find in Hungary, it was boredom. There is also a lot to see away from Lake Balaton. In this country, we were especially captivated by the sweet little towns.

Above: Breakfast at the river at Camping Mayfly in Tokaj
Below: Wine store in the city center of Tokaj

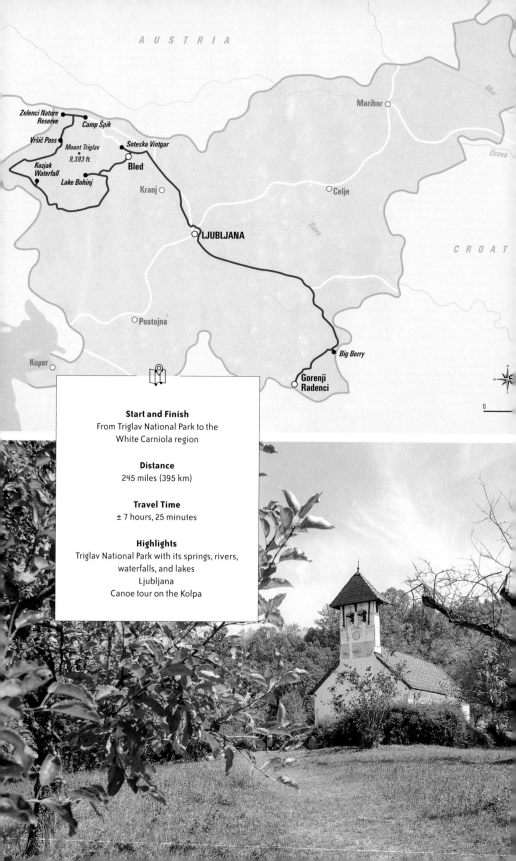

AUSTRIA

Maribor

Mur

Drava

Zelenci Nature
Reserve
Camp Špik

Vršič Pass
Mount Triglav
9,393 ft.
Soteska Vintgar

Kozjak
Waterfall
Bled

Lake Bohinj

Kranj

Celje

LJUBLJANA

Sava

CROAT

Postojna

Koper

Big Berry

Gorenji
Radenci

0

Start and Finish
From Triglav National Park to the
White Carniola region

Distance
245 miles (395 km)

Travel Time
± 7 hours, 25 minutes

Highlights
Triglav National Park with its springs, rivers,
waterfalls, and lakes
Ljubljana
Canoe tour on the Kolpa

Slovenia

HIKING AND SWIMMING IN TRIGLAV NATIONAL PARK
AND FEASTING IN LJUBLJANA

We enter Slovenia from the north and drive directly to Triglav National Park. In Camp Špik we claim a spot that is under tall trees and surrounded by mountains. In this region of Slovenia there is a lot going on. We start at the ski-jumping hill of Planica near Rateče Planica and are astounded that it is so busy here in the middle of summer. Of course, the ski jump has a special surface that allows it to be used even without snow. We watch the boys and girls during their training and then drive on.

Camp Špik
Jezerci 15, Martuljek, Slovenia, Gozd Martuljek
Phone: +386 51 63 44 66,
info@camp-spik.si
Open all year
46°29'03.8" N, 13°50'16.9" E

The source of the Sava River is close by. In Serbia we already saw how the river merges with the Danube at its end; now we are looking for its origin. We park the camper along the roadside and do our tour on foot along the fields and later through the forest of the Zelenci Nature Reserve until we reach the source. The water comes out of the earth crystal-clear and with a wonderful blue color, surrounded by bushes and with a panoramic mountain background. A really beautiful place.

On the way back, we turn into Gostilna pri Martinu, an inn with homestyle cuisine. First there are delicious main courses, but the dessert really takes the cake: a typical-for-here *kremšnita* (a vanilla-custard slice) and an order of *orehovi štruklji* (sweet-filled noodle dumplings). It is so delicious and at the same time much too much . . .

Restaurant Gostilna pri Martinu
Borovška cesta 61, Kranjska Gora, Slovenia
Phone: +386 4 582 03 00, www.julijana.info
46°29'08.0" N, 13°47'16.8" E

Pusti Gradec church in the White Carniola region

The next morning, we set out early to a day full of highlights. We drive to Kranjska Gora again but now turn onto Road 206, which takes us directly up to the Vršič Pass. A beautiful route with many spots worth seeing along the way. The first stop is the Russian Chapel. This commemorative wooden chapel is meant to memorialize the Russian prisoners of war who perished during the construction of the Vršič Pass.

The higher we go up, the more beautiful the views become. Done, we are now at the top of the pass at a height of 5,285 feet (1,611 m) above sea level. When the visibility is good, it is worth taking the twenty-minute walk to the Poštarski dom hut, at a height of 5,538 feet (1,688 m). The view of the southern slope is fantastic. But today the visibility is limited, so we drive on, now going down the southern side.

After countless hairpin curves, we finally turn right, and a few hundred yards later we can park the van. Starting here, you can go only on foot, with the appropriate shoes. First, we climb over stones and stumps up the slope, later scrambling along the stone cliff on a narrow path, holding on to the rope very tightly. Last, we climb over more rocks, and then we finally see it: far down among the rocks is the source of the Soča, the most famous river in Slovenia.

Back in our camper, we now drive along the Soča until we see a waterfall far off to the right. We park and follow the riverbed lined with white stones, and progress upstream the turquoise river. As we come around a bend in the river, the valley opens up before our eyes, and we can see all the way to the mountain beyond, and from this mountain the Boka waterfall cascades down impressively. We simply sit there, looking up, and marvel at the accidentally discovered natural beauty.

Less accidentally, we set off again on foot through the forest to the Kozjak waterfall. We came upon a picture of this waterfall during our research on Slovenia and knew right away that we wanted to go there. And now we are on our way to it. First, we must travel through the forest and then along a narrow gorge between moss-covered rocks, and finally we stand in the cave, in which, through another opening in the cave ceiling, water rushes in. We are not disappointed—the Kozjak waterfall is even more beautiful than the pictures.

We fall into bed in our campervan exhausted, but totally happy.

Top left: The traditional dessert—*kremšnita*—vanilla-custard slice
Top right: Lunch in the Slap Voje Pavel Kozelj mountain lodge
Below: Behind you can see the Boka waterfall

Slovenia and especially Triglav National Park are simply beautiful.

Camp Danica
Triglavska cesta 60, Bohinjska Bistrica
Phone: +386 574 60 10, info@camp-danica.si
Open all year
46°16′29.0″ N, 13°56′51.5″ E

But we are far from being done with Slovenia. Now we are close to Lake Bohinj, where we want to go swimming later. Now, however, a hike to a waterfall is on the agenda. Okay, maybe we don't have to look at all the waterfalls, but Steffi loves them so much, so we also march our way to the Savica waterfall. But afterward, we are going swimming—that was the deal with Lui.

The next day, Steffi announces a hike to a mountain lodge. With that, she convinces Lui immediately, and he trudges along without a murmur. Starting from Stara Fužina, we soon make our way through Mostnica Gorge. We follow the bright-turquoise, shimmering water upstream. The water masses force their way through narrow gorges, along large rocks, and over natural pools again and again. A special milestone is a rock shaped like an elephant in the river, and you can even dive under its trunk. But first we want to go up to the Slap

Voje Pavel Kozelj Inn, which more or less sits at the end of the route. We turn in here, get something to eat, and drink a beer, and only now, while we are having something cold to drink, does Steffi disclose that she wants to see the waterfall of Mostnica, a few hundred yards farther up. Strategy is important not only in sports: on the way back, Steffi dives contentedly, but it's shivering cold under the elephant trunk, and once we are back, we bathe in the much-warmer Lake Bohinj.

We get through Bled relatively quickly. Sure, the island on the lake is pretty, and the drive once around the lake is beautiful, but this is also a tourist hotspot. But the capital city of Ljubljana is something we don't want to skip. The cute little town on the Ljubljanica—yes, another river—is brimming with life. Many small cafés invite you to linger, the central market welcomes customers daily, in the old city there are many pretty buildings, and on the hill behind it stands Ljubljana Castle. Oh, we simply love this city.

Restaurant Slap Voje Pavel Kozelj
Stara Fužina 121, Bohinjsko jezero
Phone: +386 41 71 09 51,
www.slapvoje-pavel-kozelj.business.site/
46°19′45.8″ N, 13°52′40.7″ E

Above: View of Lake Bled
Below: The old city of Ljubljana

Ljubljana Resort Hotel & Camp
Dunajska cesta 270, Ljubljana
Phone: +386 70 253 845, resort@gpl.si
Open all year
46°05′51.7″ N, 14°31′05.8″ E

At the end of our tour of Slovenia, we drive to a completely different corner—to Bela krajina (also known as White Carniola), in the southeast of the country. We spent the night in Big Berry Resort, but they don't take campers anymore. An alternative could be Kanu Kamp on the Kolpa, where campervans and RVs are allowed.

Kanu Kamp Radenci ob Kolpi
Srednji Radenci 2, Stari trg ob Kolpi
Phone: +386 51 205 159,
turizem.kolpa@gmail.com
info@kolpa-adventures.com
Open from May 6 to October 6
45°27′58.0″ N, 15°05′32.9″ E

From there, we take a canoe tour on the Kolpa, which is where we see the campground. Another day we hike in Lahinja Regional Park, look for the seven springs, and pass Pusti Gradec, a small church on a hill, surrounded by a winding river. We find another beautiful spring in Semič, which is the origin of the Krupa River.

And, of course, we also go out to restaurants. The most delicious is Gostilna Muller in Črnomelj, where we sit comfortably out on the terrace.

Slovenia is really the perfect travel destination: not too far away, incredible nature with many opportunities for activities and things to see, and the perfect infrastructure for campers.

Restaurant Gostilna Muller
Ločka cesta 6, Črnomelj
Phone: +386 7 356 72 00,
www.gostilna-muller.si
45°34′02.1″ N, 15°11′37.3″ E

Above: Souvenir shop in Bela Krajina, where we baked *pogača* bread
Below: Canoe tour on the Kolpa River

POLAND

Žilina

Gerlachovský
štít
8,707 ft.

Rijo Camping Stara Lesna

Poprad

Spišský
hrad Castle

Prešov

Camping Bystrina

Chopok

Slovak Paradise
National Park

Hornád

Banská
Bystrica

Hron (Gran)

Center point of Europe

Kremnické
Bane

Hronsek

Camping Guesthouse
Sedliacky Dvor

Košice

Banská Štiavnica

Farm &
Camping Lazy

Sajó

Tisa

HUNGARY

Start and Finish
From Cerevo into Slovak Paradise National Park

Distance
314 miles (506 km)

Travel Time
± 7 hours, 30 minutes

Highlights
Farm campgrounds
Ridge walk on the Chopok
Center of Europe
Hikes in Slovak Paradise National Park

Slovakia

CUTE TOWNS, WOODEN CHURCHES,
AND COOL TOURS THROUGH THE MOUNTAINS

Once we enter Slovakia, we decide to find a comfortable spot to park and take a break for a few days. The fact that we end up at Camping Lazy—one of the best campgrounds on our whole trip—was purely by chance. Each day we get our supplies from products on the farm, look for dry wood in the forest for our campfire—because each spot has its own fire pit—and look at the farm animals. We go hiking now and then, and do, for example, a GPS hike with devices and route descriptions provided by the campground. Only after two weeks do we finally pack up our things, ready for our nineteenth country.

Farm & Camping Lazy
Cerovo 163, Cerovo
Phone: +421 908 59 08 37,
info@minicamping.eu
Open from May 1 to September 30
48°15'06.6" N, 19°13'00.4" E

First, we want to look at Banská Štiavnica. We park our campervan below the castle and set off from there on foot. Next, we look over the city rooftops from Andreja Sládkovica Street. So many different roofs—each subtly unique! We follow the street to the Námestie svätej Trojice—the Holy Trinity Square—and discover tourist information next to the Plague Column. We actually wanted only a city map but find ourselves standing in a mine shaft. The court of mines shares the same back area as the tourist information center. For only fifty cents, you can visit the mines—flashlights are provided at no charge at the tourist information center. The mine shaft shows the history and development of mining from wooden tunnels to modern caves lined with concrete.

The next destination lies a little off Road 69. The wooden church of Hronsek stands in the center of the town a little off the street and was, as many other wooden churches in Slovakia were, built under very strict rules.

Cute town in Slovakia: Banská Štiavnica

For example, everything, including load-bearing structures, had to be made of wood, and the construction had to be completed within one year. All these churches are UNESCO World Heritage Sites. The structures are impressive—with a capacity of over 1,100 people inside—but unfortunately the doors are locked.

Hronsek Wooden Church
Augusta Horislava Krc˘méryho, Hronsek
48°38′57.1″ N, 19°09′18.5″ E

We were jumping out of our seats as soon as we heard about it and are now actually driving there—to the center of Europe. We have to drive back to Zvolen and then over the E58 to get to the 65. In Kremnické Bane we turn right onto the 2504 and follow it out of the town. Somewhat on the hill, a church appears to the left, and right there at that church is the center of Europe! What a special location for us, especially since we are traveling to all forty-seven countries. Steffi—the old cynic—is not so sure about the spot and inspects very precisely the map that's hung up. And these doubts are justified—more about that in the Lithuania tour and the Ukraine chapter, because in both countries we visited other geographical centers of Europe. But no matter; it was an exciting and special moment.

Center of Europe in Slovakia
Kremnické Bane
48°44′36.8″ N, 18°54′49.6″ E

At the end of the day, we drove completely through Low Tatras National Park from south to north and park at Camping Bystrina for the night.

Camping Bystrina
Demänovská Dolina
Phone: +421 903 53 39 71,
bystrinaresort@bystrinaresort.sk
Open from May 1 to October 31
49°02′01.5″ N, 19°34′36.4″ E

Restaurant Koliba Bystrina
Right at the entrance of Camping Bystrina

But the next day, we find ourselves in the Low Tatras again. The bad weather keeps us in the lowlands for another day, but then we start our way up. We park our camper at the Biela Púť mountain station in Demänovská Dolina and put our hiking shoes on. First, we go about 3,000 feet (900 m) up over black ski slopes and straight through the forest—then we are on the Chopok at an altitude of 6,640 feet (2,024 m). Although visibility is limited, we can't get enough of the panoramic view.

Above: Wooden church of Hronsek
Below: In the middle of nature at Camping Lazy, including our own fire pit

But the actual trail starts only now—we walk along the ridge. Along the way, we get up-to-360° views; despite the icy wind, it is unbelievably beautiful up here. We first start going back down into the valley at Sedlo Pol'any. We are out for almost nine hours and understandably exhausted. There would have been a cable car up, but the feeling of having reached the top on our own cannot be replaced.

Back at Camping Bystrina, we are still able to make it into the shower and out to dinner in the neighboring restaurant, where we try the Slovak specialties *domáce halušky* (homemade spaetzle with different sauces) and *bryndzové pirohy* (filled crescent-shaped dumplings). By then, our eyes are already falling shut—and we dream about the adventures of the day.

Camping Sedliacky Dvor
Hliník 7, 97701 Brezno-Rohozná
Phone: +421 911 07 83 03,
info@sedliackydvor.com
Open from April 15 to October 31
48°47'42.7" N, 19°43'43.5" E

Camping Lazy belongs to a three-party network of Dutch campgrounds in Slovakia. The second one also lies more or less along our route, so we also drive to Camping

Guesthouse Sedliacky Dvor in Brezno. A fantastically beautiful campground awaits us here as well. The parking spots lie winding between trees and flowers, and an open hall invites communal cooking and relaxing, while chickens and cats walk over the grounds—purely idyllic.

But one highlight is still ahead of us—this national park is called Slovak Paradise, and something with a name so strong must have something to offer. We park our van at Camping Podlesok. By the way, it is definitely worth getting a hiking map of this region. Many trails are passable in only one direction, because crossing is not possible. In addition, the distances are included. We begin with the Suchá Belá hike, which starts directly next to the campground. The first part of the trail goes through the shallow riverbed: the footbridges and ladders begin later—the trail is really cool. Then, after a high ladder comes a narrow passage where we have to squeeze between rocks on flooded metal grates. This is not for the faint of heart, but we love it! After several hours, we come to the end of the gorge. The way back is then over a normal forest road.

The next day, we set out again. Today, we first follow the Prielom Hornádu, and later we turn off: it goes up again and we climb until we reach Kláštorisko.

Above: Hiking on the Chopok in the Low Tatras
Below: Hike along the ridge of the Chopok to Sedlo Pol'any
Following double page: Gloomy mood over Spišský hrad—the Spiš Castle

We don't end up looking at the ruins of the Carthusian monastery but go directly to the inn in the clearing to eat something before we start on our way back to the campground.

Camping Podlesok
Podlesok, Hrabušice
Phone: +421 53 429 91 65,
recepcia@podlesok.sk
Open all year since 2018
48°57′51.8″ N, 20°23′06.8″ E

Yes, the Slovak Paradise National Park delivers on its promise. And we only just scratched the surface. There are multiday tours that include overnight stays in huts.

On our last full day in Slovakia, we explore Levoča, a small, fine little town, and of course we can't forget Spišský hrad—the Spiš Castle. So, we drive those few miles as well.

On the way, Steffi discovers a mineral spring that shoots water through a small fountain every few minutes.

We look at the Spiš Castle only from the outside, and it is absolutely impressive. We spend our last night in the High Tatras at Rijo Camping Stara Lesna, where we once again enjoy the magnificent panorama to the fullest.

Rijo Camping Stara Lesna
Vysoké Tatry
Phone: +421 52 446 74 93,
rijocamping@rijocamping.eu
Open from May 1 to September 15
49°08′57.9″ N, 20°16′52.4″ E

Slovakia totally surprised us—not only the magnificent mountain landscapes including the Slovak Paradise, but also the cute little towns and of course the best campgrounds in Europe. Everything put together makes the perfect mix for an active vacation.

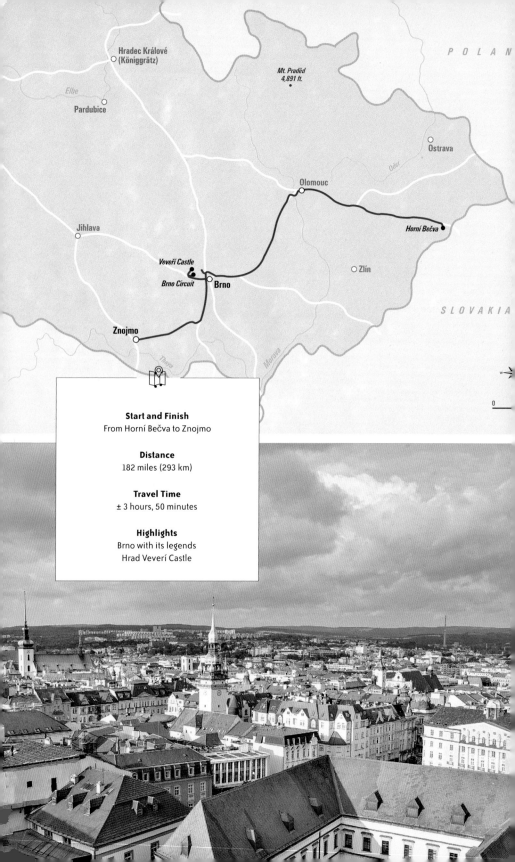

Start and Finish
From Horní Bečva to Znojmo

Distance
182 miles (293 km)

Travel Time
± 3 hours, 50 minutes

Highlights
Brno with its legends
Hrad Veverí Castle

Czech Republic

NOT TO THE CAPITAL FOR ONCE,
BUT TO BRNO AND THE SURROUNDING REGIONS

We travel into the Czech Republic from the east. This time, Prague is not the destination, even though we have been there before and we really liked the city, but it's Brno instead. Known in German as Brünn, this city is the second biggest in the Czech Republic and is the headquarters of many important public authorities.

The Czech Republic is already well known for its castles and palaces, which are the setting of countless legends and tales. Of those, there are multiple ones that belong to Brno. A crocodile hangs near the old city hall, a symbol for the evil dragon that used to live here. A cunning knight was able to put a stop to it by laying out a dead cow filled with concrete powder as bait. The dragon ate greedily, but when he drank water afterward, it burst the dragon from the inside. Steffi is an absolute fan of these legends, and so she learns at least a dozen of them after only a single day in Brno. We also look for the face of the walled-in councilman, the small leaning tower, and the Brno Wheel. There are many curiosities that can be found in the old city hall, somewhere on the building, or in the accompanying city hall tower.

At the Cabbage Market, the main square of the old city, the farmers' market is currently open. From there, we have a good view of the Moravian Museum and the Cathedral of Saints Peter and Paul behind it. We go there next and climb the good 130 steps to the viewing tower. Two terraces on opposite sides of the tower are accessible, and we can see almost all of Brno from above. Somewhat outside the city, we find Camping Hana. The sanitary facilities aren't the best, but it's fine for one night.

Camping Hana
Dlouhá 135, Veverská Bítýška
Phone: +420 733 65 74 80,
camping.hana@seznam.cz
Open from May 1 to October 1
49°16′32.2″ N, 16°27′10.7″ E

Fascinating view over Brno from the Cathedral of
Saints Peter and Paul

Today we drive to Veveří Castle, about 7 miles (12 km) from Brno. There is a tale that can be traced back to this castle that involves a prince who is lost in the woods and confronted with a violent thunderstorm. He fears for his life and prays for mercy. He says he would build a chapel and a castle here if only he comes out of it alive. He then finds the hut of a charcoal burner who gives him shelter. And we can still see today that the prince kept his promise, because Veveří Castle stands right in front of us.

The castle can be visited, and we buy ourselves tickets and pass the fortress walls through the archway. Inside, there is a large interior courtyard with different buildings, including a restaurant. We aren't hungry now, so we climb the castle wall and walk along it for a bit. We slowly see the first signs of fall. And with these, Steffi gets a headache, and she gets headaches for only one reason—a flu is coming on! Lui definitely still wants to go to the Brno Circuit. So, he takes the wheel and brings us to the racetrack.

Motorcyclists are currently training, which is no coincidence, because the Brno Circuit is used primarily for motorcycle sports. For example, the Czech Grand Prix is held here every year.

Now Steffi's strength is at its end. We find a campground near Znojmo to take a break, and days later Lui also catches the flu. So, the remaining days in the Czech Republic become relaxation days in this very well-maintained campground.

Of course, now, of all times, we have deadlines swiftly approaching. As a result, not a lot of time remains to explore the Czech Republic more extensively. But we can say one thing for sure: it doesn't always have to be Prague, even though the capital city is also very beautiful.

Camping Country
Hluboké Mašůvky 257, Hluboké Mašůvky
Tel. +420 515 25 52 49,
camping-country@cbox.cz
Open from May 1 to October 31
48°55'14.1"N 16°01'30.8"E

Veveří Castle
Veverská Bítýška-Bisterz
49°15'23.4" N, 16°27'37.6" E

Brno Circuit
Masarykův okruh 201, Ostrovačice
49°12'13.2" N, 16°26'42.9" E

Above: Motorcycle race on the Brno Circuit
Below: On the grounds of Veveří Castle

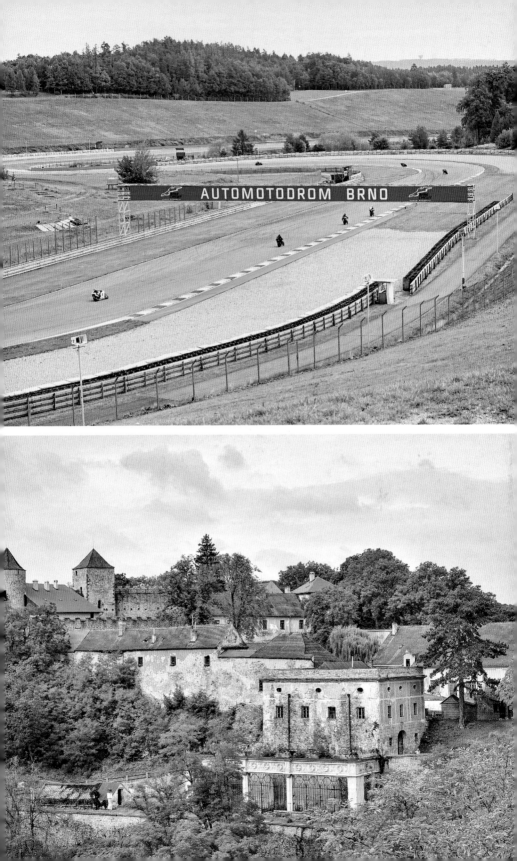

Start and Finish
From Melk to Spielberg

Distance
227 miles (446 km)

Travel Time
± 6 hours, 10 minutes

Highlights
Route along the Danube with Krems
Melk Abbey
Swimming lakes
Graz
Winterleiten in Zirbenland

Austria

ALONG THE DANUBE
TO KREMS AND MELK

We enter Austria coming from the Czech Republic. Krems, on the Danube, is a place we want to look at, but we can't simply take a car park ticket here—instead, we must buy several paper slips at a *Trafik* (kiosk), according to our desired parking time, and enter the date, including our arrival time, by hand. A gentleman passing by explained everything to us clearly.

We pass through the city gate to enter the beautiful old city of Krems and meander through the streets, with colorful homes decorated with flowers, until we reach the cathedral in Wachau. We also take a peek inside. We stroll leisurely back to the camper and then keep driving upstream along the Danube but end up switching to the other side of the bank because it is supposed to be prettier for the next stage of the drive. Along the way, we come upon Camping Rossatzbach and spend the rest of the day watching ships directly on the Danube.

Camping Rossatzbach
Rossatzbach 21, Rossatzbach
Phone: +43 676 848 81 48 00,
www.wachaucamping-rossatz.at
Open from March 1 to October 31
48°23'28.2" N, 15°30'59.2" E

High above the Danube lie the castle ruins of Aggstein. We look at them today, even though the weather is a typical autumn day. The grounds themselves are already really an eye-catcher, but the view surpasses everything. We can see the Danube extend continuously below us. And if the mythological term "Nibelung" means anything to you, you can tour a comprehensive exhibit in the basement.

Not too much farther along the Danube is the town of Melk, including the Melk Abbey. The Benedictine monastery is probably a familiar name to many. We park directly in front in the large parking lot and explore the monastery grounds on foot. If you buy a ticket, you can also look at the building and the gardens, but even without a ticket we are able to see a lot of the impressive compound.

Above: Clock tower as the landmark of Graz
Middle: Steffi and Lui in Graz
Below: In the inner courtyard of the Benedictine monastery Melk Abbey

A few very warm days follow, which is why we first visit a few swimming lakes before we head off to Graz. We come across the reservoir swimming lake of Rechnitz—a comfortably cool lake surrounded by a lawn. We check in later to Camping Steinmann in Stubenberg am See, where we of course also end up in the lake.

Camping & Gasthof Steinmann
Buchberg 85, Stubenberg am See
Phone: +43 3176 83 90,
office@stubenberg-camping.at
Open all year
47°13′58.1″ N, 15°48′19.1″ E

But enough laziness—today the city of Graz is on the agenda, where we luckily find a parking spot on the side of the road. For the first time in over nine months on the road, we find ourselves in a city in which there is almost no way to park other than in a parking garage. But enough of that: we start walking toward the city center, get ourselves a city map at the tourist information center, and receive a few tips there as well. In the main square (Hauptplatz), the heart of Graz, our city tour starts according to the information brochure. We inspect the facade of the building at the corner of Sporgasse and Hauptplatz very minutely, and yes, we discover the noses and mouths hidden among the flower garlands in the facade.

In the bakery Hofbäckerei Edegger-Tax on Hofgasse Street, which has been deemed a UNESCO World Heritage Site, we try the very sweet *Sissi-Busserl*. We also pass the double-spiral staircase, which is a very funny-looking piece of masonry artwork from the past. In the affectionately named Bermuda Triangle District (Bermuda-Dreieck Viertel), there are especially many bars and restaurants, which is why you can get lost for hours on end around the Färberplatz. The same thing happens to us, and we land happily in the beer garden at Glöckl Bräu for lunch.

Restaurant Glöckl Bräu
Glockenspielplatz 2-3, Graz
Phone: +43 316 81 47 81, www.gloecklbraeu.at
Open daily from 9:00 a.m. to 11:30 p.m.
47°04′16.7″ N, 15°26′28.1″ E

Next, we take a stroll along the Mur, the river of the city of Graz, to aid in our digestion, and come across Mur Island. From there, it's not much farther until we reach the landmark symbol of Graz, the clocktower. Cable car, stairs, elevator—there are many ways to reach the top of the castle hill. From there we have a terrific view over the city, with a population of 435,000. Afterward, we spot it: the famous clocktower, whose clock has been telling time since 1712. We go back down the back of the mountain on foot, back into the old city, and back to our camper.

Above: High above the Danube: the castle ruins of Aggstein
Below: Mountain lake of Winterleiten in Zirbenland

Since we want to see Spielberg tomorrow, including the racetrack, we decide to stay at Camping Murinsel. What a terrific decision! The parking spots are located around a large swimming pond, the infrastructure and service are fantastic, and there is even a second, smaller pond for dogs.

Camping Murinsel
Teichweg 1, Großlobming
Phone: +43 664 304 50 45,
office@camping-murinsel.at
Open one week before Easter until October 31
47°11'43.1" N, 14°48'09.4" E

The Red Bull Ring is calling, and of course it's a call that Lui cannot ignore. The racetrack even scores points with Steffi because we don't have to stand just along the fence, but we can actually be in the paddock during the training races and can get really close to the track.

But above all, we traveled to this region due to a travel acquaintance we met at the Black Sea. The couple, whom we met there multiple times, show us their home, accompanied by their son. In the beautiful old town of Judenburg, we eat delicious ice cream, and then we drive up to Winterleiten in Zirbenland, where we take a small hike around the mountain lake. In the Winterleitenhütte restaurant, we are spoiled with a platter of cold specialties, called a Brettljause, and afterward the son plays us a march on his Styrian harmonica—a next-level experience and the crowning conclusion to our tour of Austria.

Restaurant Winterleitenhütte
Ossach 45, Ossach
Phone: +43 3578 82 10, www.winterleiten.com
47°05'39.6" N, 14°34'16.1" E

Above: One of the many swimming lakes we visited due to the heat
Below: Inn in Krems on the Danube

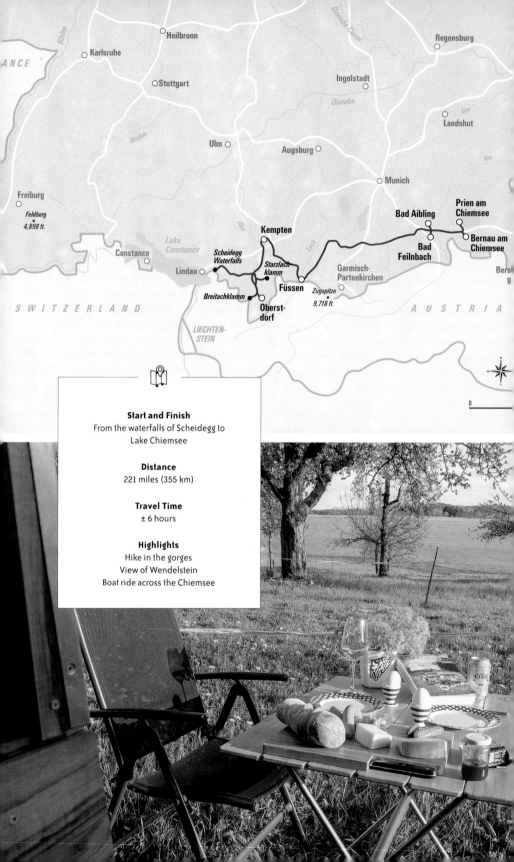

Heilbronn

Karlsruhe

ANCE

Stuttgart

Regensburg

Danube Canal

Ingolstadt

Danube

Landshut

Ulm

Augsburg

Isar

Freiburg

Feldberg
4,898 ft.

Lake
Constance

Munich

Bad Aibling

Prien am
Chiemsee

Kempten

Constance

Lindau

Scheidegg
Waterfalls

Starzlach-
klamm

Lech

Füssen

Breitachklamm

Oberst-
dorf

Zugspitze
9,718 ft.

Garmisch-
Partenkirchen

Bad
Feilnbach

Bernau am
Chiemsee

Berc
g

SWITZERLAND

LIECHTEN-
STEIN

AUSTRIA

0

Start and Finish
From the waterfalls of Scheidegg to
Lake Chiemsee

Distance
221 miles (355 km)

Travel Time
± 6 hours

Highlights
Hike in the gorges
View of Wendelstein
Boat ride across the Chiemsee

Germany

ALONG THE ALPINE ROAD
THROUGH BAVARIA TO THE CHIEMSEE

On our tour through Germany, we dedicate ourselves to the south: the journey goes from Allgäu to the Chiemsee-Alpine region. We are traveling with the book *Landvergnügen* (*Country Pleasure*), which allows us to find terrific agricultural farms to spend the night at. These farms tend not to be public but are reserved for users of *Landvergnügen*, which is why we are writing down only the town we spend the night in.

Coming from Lake Constance, we spend the night in Opfenbach, idyllically on a cow pasture, before we go to see the waterfalls of Scheidegg on our first real travel day. We must pay a small fee, then we can see the waterfalls that flow over two levels. They are nice but don't overly excite us. The old city of Wangen is more up our alley. Buildings such as the Ravensburger Tor gate tower and the city hall are beautiful, and many of the homes from the Middle Ages are decorated with murals. After a delicious lunch,

we drive to the next place to spend the night, which is also a public location. We park next to the farm on an unmown lawn with a fantastic view of the Alps.

Kohler Organic Farm (Bio-Hof Kohler)
Wolfertshofen 1, Heimenkirch
Phone: +49 8381 928 29 44,
Landvergnügen & Park4Night
47°38′22.4″ N, 9°55′31.2″ E

The next morning, we drive to Breitachklamm and first learn in the parking lot that the gorge is currently closed due to clearing work. It's a shame—the hike along the river is supposed to be gorgeous. The Starzlachklamm is supposed to be a close alternative, or so we thought, until we start walking from the parking lot. Soon we reach a sign that says that there is also a closure due to bad weather.

Breakfast on a farm, using *Landvergnügen*

We can still reach the entrance to the gorge, so we are at least able to walk through a little of the landscape. We spent the night on an Icelandic horse farm, and yes, Steffi disappeared for hours.

The weather is not so good today, perfect for a city stroll through Kempten and freshly prepared *Kässpätzle* (egg noodles with cheese) from a market stand on the Residenzplatz square. Later we make our way through Füssen, another beautiful little town with terrific houses from the Middle Ages. As for Neuschwanstein Castle, we just pass by. It was already clear to us that there were going to be a lot of people there, but it is still a beautiful castle, and we want to at least see it from the outside with our own eyes.

Even though the weather isn't going to boost our mood, some cake has a pretty good chance. The historic Café Winklstüberl is inland and is known for its homemade cakes far and wide. We can barely decide—it's a paradise for people with a sweet tooth, and the cakes we picked out are delicious. Kaiser Camping lies only a few miles back in the valley, which is where we stay for a few nights.

The following days we hike leisurely from the campground to the Sterntaler Filze, a natural bog landscape, from which peat was harvested in earlier times. Beautifully designed hiking and themed trails lead us through the natural landscape, and informational signs explain what used to be done here.

After another night in Kaiser Camping, the weather is finally better, and we take the cogwheel railway up to the Wendelstein at an altitude of 6,030 feet (1,838 m). There is a lot of snow at the top, which is why the route to the actual peak and the panorama route are closed. The view over the mountains into the valley is clear and magnificent. Even the ride with the cogwheel railway is an experience—the views are terrific and the incline is outrageously steep, and we are really pressed into our seats.

After arriving back at the bottom, we drive to Prien on Lake Chiemsee and let the day come to an end in the sauna area of the Prienavera Adventure Pool (Erlebnisbades Prienavera). We already parked our van in front of the wellness spa at Camping Harras, directly on the lake.

Kaiser Camping Outdoor Resort
Reithof 2, Bad Feilnbach
Phone: +49 8066 88 44 00,
info@kaiser-camping.com
Open all year
47°38'22.4" N, 9°55'31.2" E

Above: Parking spot at Kohler Organic Farm, with a view of the Alps
Below: The Ravensburger Tor gate in Wangen in Allgäu
Following double page: With rental bikes on the "King's Tour" around Lake Chiemsee

Panorama Camping Harras
Harrasser Str. 135, Prien am Chiemsee
Tel. +49 8051 90 46 13,
info@camping-harras.de
Open from April 12 to October 31
47°50'25.3"N 12°22'24.7"E

Another beautiful day invites us to a boat ride on Lake Chiemsee. We board in Prien and let ourselves rock over the lake and get out at the island Frauenchiemsee. Beautiful homes with enchanting gardens await us on the island tour. We try a smoked whitefish, the local specialty, at Gürtler Fischer garden restaurant and find it to be very delicious.

Back on the boat, we ride to Herreninsel island. There we walk to the Herrenchiemsee New Palace; the enormous park in front of the ostentatious palace is already very impressive. With a tour we are able to see a few rooms inside the building and see the similarity of the palace to Versailles much more clearly. We let the evening come to an end at Camping Harras, directly on Lake Chiemsee.

The next day is not as sunny, perfect for a bike tour. In Bernau am Chiemsee, we rent two e-Bikes at the bike rental shop Fritz Müller and go on the "King's Tour," which is the route that goes all the way around the lake. We ride as close to the bank as possible counterclockwise around the lake and pass by beautiful green areas but also through smaller towns. The so-called Malerwinkel (painter's angle) between Seebruck and Gstadt invites us to stay awhile with dreamlike panoramas over the lake and mountains.

Start and Finish
From St. Gallen to the Furka Pass

Distance
159 miles (256 km)

Travel Time
± 5 hours, 10 minutes

Highlights
St. Gallen
Appenzell
Tamina Gorge
Rhine Gorge
Oberalp and Furka Passes

SWITZERLAND AND THE PRINCIPALITY OF LIECHTENSTEIN

Switzerland and the Principality of *Liechtenstein*

ALONG THE GRAND TOUR OF SWITZERLAND
OVER PASSES AND LAKES AS WELL AS THROUGH LIECHTENSTEIN

We start our tour through Switzerland in St. Gallen. The Gallus City is located far in the east, and beautiful historic buildings line the streets of the old town. We stroll past the textile museum along Multergasse, one of the main shopping streets in the city. In Spisergasse, it became quickly clear to us why St. Gallen is called the "City of Bay Windows." All the bay windows are unique and very beautiful. We enter the monastery courtyard from the rear and now are standing in the middle of the Abbey District, a UNESCO World Heritage Site. We view the cathedral, which is especially beautiful on the inside, and the abbey library as well, with its unbelievably impressive baroque hall. So much culture is making us hungry, and even there, St. Gallen has a special tradition: the St. Galler bratwurst (the larger variety is also known as OLMA-Bratwurst) as well as the St. Galler *stumpen* (a type of sausage). You can find these two specialties, for example, in the Marktplatz (market square) at Metzgerei Rietmann (butcher shop) to take with you hot right away in the middle of the day. And take note: it is scandalous to eat a St. Galler sausage with mustard. Steffi stays true to the custom, while Lui—when no one is looking—reaches for the mustard anyway.

After our snack, we drive out of the city and into the rolling green, hilly landscape. We follow the brown signs for the Grand Tour of Switzerland, an approximately 1,000-mile (1,600 km) route to the most-beautiful corners of Switzerland. The next destination is Appenzell. Far outside the town we already see the characteristic wooden farmhouses. We park our camper in a spot on the Zielstrasse and go on foot to the center. The colorfully painted wooden houses create the typical townscape, along with traditional items such as leather belts with cows on them, Appenzeller herbal schnapps, and Appenzeller cheese, which is also available as a fondue.

Above: Stroll through the old town of St. Gallen
Below: Freestanding spot on the Furka Pass

Further following the Grand Tour of Switzerland, we are led farther up the street until we park on the Schwägalp Pass and are now standing at the base of Säntis. Looking out from the 8,205-foot (2,501 m) mountain, you can look out not only over Switzerland, but also into all the five neighboring countries—if the visibility is good. A cable car can bring guests up to the top of the highest mountain in the Alpstein massif in ten minutes. We decide to hike on the Schwägalp Pass.

In the evening we look for a place to spend the night shortly before Vaduz, where we end up spending a quiet night in the forest.

**Freestanding spot in the forest
near the Rhine**
Forest parking lot near Sargans, close to the
Rhine (Park4Night)
47°02′51.0″ N, 9°28′28.2″ E

Switzerland and the Principality of Liechtenstein may be different countries, but they are still connected by a lot—not only the Swiss franc, which is also the official currency of Liechtenstein. We go through Vaduz with a great attention to detail and stroll through the streets, and we are astounded by the number of visitors from Asia. We get our passports stamped for fun in the tourist information center before we look at the Liechtenstein National Museum and the Treasure Chamber (Schatzkammer des Fürsten). In the end we walk up to Vaduz Castle, the official residence of the Prince of Liechtenstein which cannot be toured but is worth the walk for the beautiful view from above.

Later we drive our campervan up the Liechtenstein mountains until we reach Malbun. Everything is still closed because of the preseason, so we just have a picnic at the Gänglesee lake.

Back in Switzerland, our first destination of the day is the Tamina Gorge. Starting in Bad Ragaz, we walk through the forest to Alten Bad Pfäfers, the oldest baroque bathhouse in Switzerland, which is used as a restaurant today. After the bridge, we follow the turnstile entrance to the Tamina Gorge. For this, we need five francs per person in coins, which we throw in the machine for the entrance fee. One path runs along the cliff walls; below us the wild Tamina flows, and above us the cliff walls are so close to each other that we can only rarely see up to the sky. Ultimately, we reach the source, whose thermal waters are still used today in the baths of Bad Ragaz.

In Landquart we leave the Grand Tour of Switzerland route and drive over Chur to Bonaduz, where we turn onto a small street to Versam.

Above: Picnic at Gänglesee lake in the Principality of Liechtenstein
Below: The residence of the Prince of Liechtenstein, Castle Vaduz

The route leads us along the Vorderrhein, and soon we get spectacular views from the viewing platforms of Zault and Spitg into the Rhine Gorge. In Versam itself, we get information at the small visitor center and learn about the Rhine Gorge Bus, which takes hikers back to the exit after a tour of the gorge or can be used directly as a sightseeing bus. We have our mobile base with us already, so we drive with the van to the Islabord observation deck. The view to the gorge is terrific—below, a few people are paddling on the river in rafting boats. The view from even farther up is more spectacular, which we can enjoy only thanks to a drone. Like a picture book, the turquoise river meanders around the white limestone cliffs. So, this is what it looks like—the Grand Canyon of Switzerland.

We park the campervan again in Valendas and start on a walk at the big wooden fountain with its mermaid. We fill our bottles with cold drinking water here—every fountain in Switzerland is supplied with drinking water unless something on the fountain says explicitly otherwise. Right next to it is a small, free museum. During the tour we notice the treasure map of Alix von Faszinatur, with a scavenger hunt for children. We need to find out why the mermaid is no longer in her spot on the fountain. We follow the trail and stock up on

some bread, salami, and cheese in a small farm shop, and then we are ready for our walk. This tour is worth it even without kids: it leads us once again over the Rhine Gorge and to the Alix viewing platform, where we have a picnic. We were walking for only about an hour, so there is still enough time to see a proper pass.

We follow the Vorderrhein farther west, and after Sedrun the first winding roads begin, which lead us up to spectacular views of the valley at an elevation of 6,706 feet (2,044 m) at the top of the Oberalp Pass. This is what we know and love about Switzerland—only mountains surrounding us, a small mountain lake, and the opportunity to hike for hours. We find a spot for the campervan where we can also spend the night and set off on foot to explore the mountain world. Starting from here, it is also possible to hike to the source of the Rhine, which is something we definitely want to do another time if the opportunity presents itself.

Freestanding spot at the Oberalp Pass
Top of the Oberalp Pass at an altitude of over 6,706 feet (2,004 m) (Park4Night)
46°39′44.4″ N, 8°40′15.0″ E

Above: Hiking trail through Valendas, with the small farm shop to the left
Below: Ruinaulta, otherwise known as the Rhine Gorge

Our next destination lies between Andermatt and Göschenen. Steffi knows the Schöllenen Gorge from a radio drama from her childhood. Apparently, the devil personally built a bridge over the raging river Reuss. As payment, he claimed the first soul to cross the bridge, so the resourceful villagers decided to send an old billy goat. In actuality, merchants used to pass through here in earlier times with their livestock because—thanks to this bridge—it was the quickest way over the Alps. To be able to stand here and look at the Devil's Bridge (Teufelsbrücke) is really something special.

Starting at Andermatt, we follow the Grand Tour of Switzerland once again. The Furka Pass lies ahead of us. And with it there are many winding and steep roads, but our Opel Monavo does well with them. It also gets a lot of breaks because we keep stopping and enjoying the views. We decide, as we finally arrive at the top of the pass at an elevation of 7,976 feet (2,431 m), that we want to spend another night at this lofty height. But we first drive a few hundred yards down the western side of the pass. In the parking lot near Hotel Belvedere, we put on our hiking shoes and set off at the end of the parking lot. The Rhône Glacier can be reached from here with the most unusual ice grotto in Europe: a tunnel not quite 328 feet (100 m) long that leads into the glacier. Wow, this is just insanely beautiful and ice cold at the same time.

After this experience we drive to a quieter parking spot back toward the top of the pass and watch the groundhogs. During the night we are thoroughly shaken. The weather up here in the mountains is significantly rougher than in the midlands.

Freestanding spot at the Furka Pass
Top of the Furka Pass at an altitude of over 7,976 feet (2,431 m) (Park4Night)
46°34′18.0″ N, 8°24′40.0″ E

We would like to follow the Grand Tour of Switzerland farther: the Aletsch Glacier, the beautiful Valais, and western Switzerland come next, but time doesn't allow it, and we have to turn around.

There is one thing we have learned about our home country yet again: Switzerland is beautiful and offers scenic highlights not far away from each other, and a dream route along the Grand Tour that is guaranteed not to forgo any attraction. Sure, the prices are higher than in the surrounding countries, but it's possible to park pretty much anywhere in the open, which allows your travel costs to be lowered significantly.

Above: On the Grand Tour of Switzerland, with a view of the Säntis
Below: The colorful wooden houses of Appenzell

Mont Blanc
15,771 ft.

Aix-les-Bains

Lyon

Clermont-Ferrand

oges

Puy de Sancy
6,188 ft.

St. Étienne

Grenoble

Barre des
Écrins
13,458 ft.

ITALY

Mt. Lozère
5,584 ft.

Rhône

Mont
Ventoux
6,263 ft.

Tarn

Nîmes

Avignon

Toulouse

Montpellier

Aix-en-Provence

Camargue

Durance

Verdon Gorge

Nice MONACO

Cannes

Port Grimaud

Marseillan
Plage

Marseille

La Ciotat

Toulon

Gulf of Lion

Villefranche-
de-Conflent

Perpignan

Mediterranean

Sea

Start and Finish
From Aix-les-Bains nach Villefranche-de-Conflent

Distance
714 miles (1,149 km)

Travel Time
± 14 hours, 55 minutes

Highlights
Gorges du Verdon
Port Grimaud
Camargue Regional Natural Park
Villefranche-de-Conflent

France and Monaco

THROUGH THE GRAND CANYON OF EUROPE
AND ALONG THE MEDITERRANEAN COAST INTO THE PYRENEES

France is a paradise for campers of all preferences—open air, campground, parking spots: everything is possible. And we finally attached solar panels to our roof, allowing us to be self-sufficient in our travels. We then spend the first night freestanding in Aix-les-Bains before we drive farther toward the Gorges du Verdon the next day.

Freestanding spot in Aix-le-Bains
Parking spot on the lake (Park4Night)
45°42′0.1″ N, 5°53′8.8″ E

On the way to the Verdon Gorge, we come upon the Gorges de la Méouge and drive along it: a really beautiful gorge with terrific views of the river and the surrounding rocks. We take the country road, since we're not in any rush, and drive past lavender fields, and in the evening we find a nice parking spot in Riez on the outskirts of the town, from which we can go into the center of the town comfortably on foot.

Parking spot: Aire de Camping-Car Riez
Rue du Faubourg Saint-Sébastien (Park4Night)
43°49′20.2″ N, 6°05′32.6″ E

Before we finally arrive at the Gorges du Verdon the next day, we make a stop in Moustiers-Sainte-Marie. We did it only because the tourist information center for the region is located there, but the town itself is worth a visit in its own right. It is so pretty.

And then we drive to the Verdon Natural Regional Park, past the man-made Lake of Sainte-Croix, and into the Verdon Gorge. During the summer, you can take a canoe out on the turquoise-colored water, but now there is already snow lying in the shaded areas. The nature in late fall, with its bright colors, is really beautiful, with this wide view over the gorge. We leave the D952 in La Palud-sur-Verdon and turn onto the smaller D23.

Breakfast at the ocean in La Ciotat

It's a circular route that can be completely driven only in the clockwise direction, with really beautiful views over the Verdon Gorge. For us, it is too cold to spend the night in the mountains, so we drive an hour farther south and are in Nice. We spend the night there outside the city, at Camping Park Maurettes.

Camping Park Maurettes
730 Avenue du Dr Julien Lefebvre,
Villeneuve-Loubet
Phone: +33 4 93 20 91 91,
info@parcdesmaurettes.com
Open all year
43°37'51.6" N, 7°07'47.1" E

Our twenty-fifth country is now only a few miles away, and still it is difficult to find a parking spot there for a vehicle that's 9.5 feet high (2.90 m). Of course, we drive to Monaco. The street M6007—Avenue Bella Vista—takes us to our destination and is a panoramic road at the same time. The views of the coast and the ocean are magnificent. And then we finally find an underground parking garage that is specially intended for campers and other large vehicles, and there is exactly one free spot left. Perfect!

Parking des Ecoles
(Underground parking garage for campers)
3 Avenue des Guelfes, Monaco
43°43'35.5" N, 7°25'00.9" E

We explore the city center of the second-smallest country in the world and go up to the Prince's Palace, where we can look down upon Port Hercules. That is where the start/finish line of the Monaco Grand Prix is located. From the palace, we stroll through the old town located in front of it, which has the name "Fürstenbezirk" (Princedom). We take the stairs down the hill and stroll slowly back to the parking garage. We spent the night in France again and even had to drive a considerable distance until we reached the parking spot at Sainte-Maxime.

Aire de Camping-Car Sainte-Maxime
67 D25, Sainte-Maxime (Park4Night)
43°19'02.0" N, 6°37'48.8" E

The next day we explore Port Grimaud, a part of Grimaud that is made up of many canals. We stroll through the streets on foot, past the small shops, and up to the old lighthouse. A pretty place that recalled memories of past vacations. In the evening, we find a nice freestanding spot in La Ciotat on a rarely traveled street directly on the ocean, where we watch the sun set on the cliffs (prohibited today).

Above: View over Monaco
Below: The port of Port Grimaud

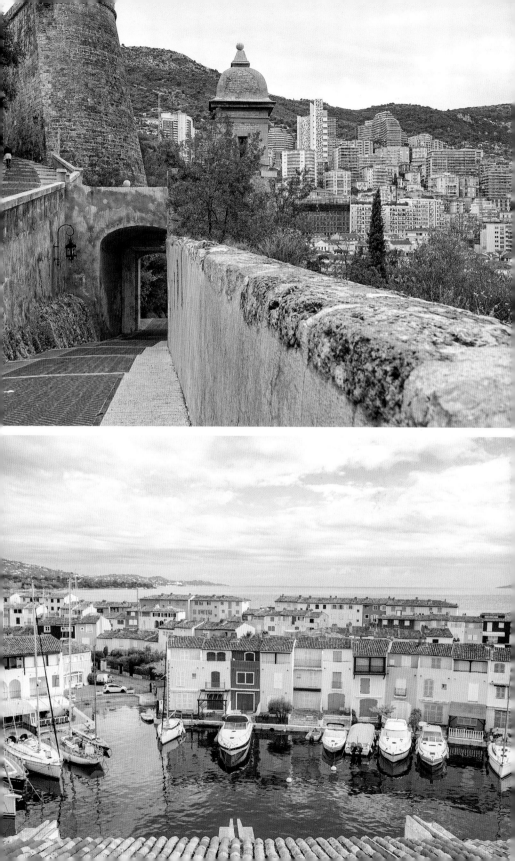

Alternative freestanding spot in La Ciotat
1-17 Avenue du Capitaine Marchand, La Ciotat
43°10′04.8″ N, 5°36′17.5″ W

Jacob's Boulangerie
35 Rue Bédarrides, Aix-en-Provence
43°31′42.2″ N, 5°26′50.8″ E

Coincidentally, there is a market in Aix-en-Provence that day, and of course Steffi starts beaming with delight when we learn this upon our arrival. That completes our day—we stroll through the stands and test a few local specialties directly in the market. Lui treats himself later to a duck sandwich from Jacob's Boulangerie.

Unfortunately, we have heard a lot about significant safety issues in Camargue Regional Natural Park. We want to go there; however, we are not interested in freestanding in such an area. That is why we drive to Camping Neptun, and soon after arriving in the evening we get neighbors with a smashed window. They were hiking in the Camargue, but when they came back to their camper, it was cleaned out.

Camping Neptune
4 Allée Gustave Eiffel,
Saint-Mitre-les-Remparts
Phone: +33 4 42 44 06 60,
campingneptune@wanadoo.fr
Open all year
43°28'04.8" N, 5°01'09.5" E

But there are flamingos there, and of course the Camargue horses! Steffi will not part with her plan despite the safety concerns, so we drive into the natural park the next morning. Our compromise is as follows—we will see only as much as we can see from the street or from where we can also see the camper. So, this is how we experience a really terrific day in the Camargue, seeing many flamingos from the Route de Fielouse road and discovering the white Camargue horses in a field as well, and even the black bulls. We even do a small hike one by one near the visitor center inside the park. We slept a little farther southwest at a parking spot in Marseillan Plage, of course with an extensive walk on the beach before breakfast.

On a walk through the Natural Reserve Bagnas, which begins almost right next to our parking spot, we discover many flamingos once again.

Aire de Camping-Car Marseillan Plage
4 Rue des Goélands, Marseillan (Park4Night)
43°19'09.7" N, 3°32'53.6" E

We are slowly approaching Spain, and with that, our next country of travel where we want to go up in the Pyrenees. As we drive through the foothills, a particularly beautiful place catches our interest, and we park our campervan. We have landed in Villefrance-de-Conflent. The impressive city walls come out of the time of the conflict between Spain and France. Within the wall, stone homes with really cool store signs are hiding. It's exciting to see what you can discover on the roadside.

We wanted to spend the last night in France freestanding, but up here in the Pyrenees it's already very cold during the day. So, we check into Camping La Griole. This night will stay in our memory for a long time, because while closing, the whole side door falls off. Thanks to the help of a tinsmith who lived at the campground, we are able to forcefully get the door back on the track, but it has to be urgently repaired the next day.

Camping La Griole
39 Route de l'Andorre,
Targassonne (Park4Night)
Phone: +33 4 68 30 03 84,
www.lagriole.com
Open all year
Ownership change in 2022—check the
website before arriving
42°29'45.1" N, 1°59'09.2" E

So, our French adventure ends with a great scare. Nevertheless, for us, France is one of the best travel destinations for a camper. In almost every town there is place to park: we have discovered a really cool app, Park4Night, and now with solar panels, we can enjoy our newfound freedom at once. Yes, we really like France.

Previous double page: Flamingos in Camargue
Regional Natural Park
Above: Love at first sight in the Verdon Gorge
Below: Viewing platform in the Camargue

Start and Finish
From the border at Sant Julià to Soldeu

Distance
18 miles (40 km)

Travel Time
± 40 minutes

Highlights
Cheap gas
Old city of Andorra la Vella
Surrounding mountains

Pic de Tristaina
9,442 ft.

El Serrat

Pic de l'Estanyó
9,554 ft.

Canillo

Soldeu

ANDORRA LA VELLA

Valira d'Orient

FRANCE

Pic dels Pessons
9,400 ft.

Les Escaldes

St. Julia de Lòria

Gran Valira

SPAIN

Duana de Sant Julià de Lòria

0   3 mi.

Andorra

A TAX HAVEN
IN THE MIDDLE OF THE MOUNTAINS

You tend to hear two things about Andorra: tax-free shopping and cheap gas. With these things in mind, we arrive at the border and take part in a statistical survey from the monarchy about our purposes of entry, making our first stop at a gas station. A liter of diesel costs only 0.97 euros (approximately 3.66 euros per gallon), so it's a little cheaper than in Catalonia, where we paid around 1.09 euros per liter (4.12 euros per gallon).

A difference between Monaco and Andorra is that Andorra is not a city-state but is home to forty-four municipalities and by size is the largest microstate in Europe. First, we explore the capital city of Andorra la Vella, about 3,300 feet (1,000 m) above sea level. We make our way along the streets and visit the Church of Saint Stephen, even though tourists are allowed in only during July and August. Well, then only from the outside for us. We also look at the Casa de la Vall only from the outside and take more time to explore the pedestrian zone instead.

Àrea d'autocaravanes
River Centre Comercial, CG1 s/n,
Sant Julià de Lòria (Park4Night)
42°27'12.9" N, 1°29'10.3" E

In the evening, we park our campervan with a few other campers in a supermarket parking lot, which even has a disposal center. Not pretty, but at least we found a spot. Even the Wi-Fi signal reaches out to here, but careful—Andorra is not a member of the EU, even though you pay in euros. With this one night spent in the country, we end up being there twice as long as the usual tourist, who normally stays for only one day.

On the second day we dedicate ourselves to the surrounding area. We follow the street GC-2 to Soldeu and can look upon the capital from a little farther away. Only then do we first notice how far among the mountains this country lies.

Top right: On the road in the mountains of Andorra
Top left: Border crossing to Andorra
Below: View into the valley of Andorra la Vella

There are various ski areas—for example, on the Pic Negre, where ski lifts bring experienced skiers up to elevations of 9,226 feet (2,812 m).

But during the wintertime, the difficult entry into Andorra keeps most winter sportsmen away. Entry is possible only from the north over high passes, and coming from Barcelona means an almost 125-mile (200 km) detour for us living in central Europe. So, the microstate of Andorra remains just a shopping paradise, for us, and even we will probably not be in Andorra again anytime soon simply due to the entry difficulties.

The Cathedral of Saint Stephen in the center of Andorra la Vella

Praia das Catedrais
(Beach of the Cathedrals)   Bay of Biscay   F R A N C E

Santander   Donostia-
Gijón   Deba   San Sebastián
Bilbao
León   Pamplona   ANDORRA
Vigo   Bardenas
Ourense   Reales
Valladolid   Ebro
Porto   Duero   Barcelona
Zaragoza
Atlantic
Ocean   MADRID
Balearic Islands
PORTUGAL   Mallo
Valencia   Ibiza
Lisbon   Badajoz   Formentera
Guadiana   Alicante
Guadalquivir   Mediterranean Se
Sevilla   Tabernas
El Rocío   Granada
Lagos   Gulf of Cádiz   Antequera   Cabo de Gata
Cádiz   Málaga   Frigiliana
Vejer de la Frontera   Casares
Tarifa
0

Start and Finish
From Zaragoza to Ourense and from El Rocío to
the Tabernas Desert

Distance
1,146 miles (1,845 km)

Travel Time
± 22 hours, 30 minutes

Highlights
Bardenas Reales badlands
Pamplona
Gijon
Praia das Catedrais
El Rocío
White villages in Andalucia

Spain

THROUGH THE BADLANDS AND ALONG THE NORTHERN COAST
TO ANDALUCIA WITH ITS WHITE VILLAGES

Spain is a land of contrasts, and we want to see them all, starting far in the north. First stop: Zaragoza! The city on the Ebro has a city center worth visiting. We cross the Puente del Piedra on foot to reach the old city, look at the impressive Basilíca del Pilar, and stroll through the streets. We leave the city in the afternoon and drive to Arguedas. There is a parking spot there directly at the Cuevas de Arguedas—abandoned cave dwellings.

Area de autocaravanes Argueidas
65 Calle Val, Arguedas (Park4Night)
42°10'25.9" N, 1°35'29.9" W

The next day we drive into the Bardenas Reales badlands. Coming from Arguedas, we first stop at the visitor center, where we also get a map of the park. We drive through the park on good dirt roads, past spectacular rock formations such as the Castilldetierra, the famous rock columns with "heads." The surreal landscape fascinates us and leaves

a deep impression. Unfortunately, it is not possible to stay here overnight, so we leave the Bardenas Reales in the evening and find another free parking spot in Olito.

Area de autocaravanes Olite
9 Paseo de Doña Leonor, Olite (Park4Night)
42°28'48.9" N, 1°38'50.4" W

We follow the N-121 until we reach Pamplona, a city best known for its Running of the Bulls. There is not much of that to see, but we find that good. Pamplona itself is quite pretty to look at. We stroll through the alleys, and in doing so we pass multiple city gates and can see the city wall in the Corralillos del Gas, the fighting animal stables during the Festival of San Fermín (always from July 6 to 14). The city only really starts to come to life in the evening. The many bars put tables outside, people are drinking, and of course there are plenty of *tapas*, which are called *pintxos* here in the north.

The Castilldetierra rock formations in the
Bardenas Reales

Parking autocaravanes
Trinitarios Pamplona
Av. de Gipuzkoa Etorbidea,
1–409, Pamplona
(Park4Night)
42°49'15.7" N, 1°39'23.5" W

After spending two nights in the parking spot in Pamplona, we are drawn to the ocean. We follow the A15 to Donostia-San Sebastián, where we turn off and continue following the coast, until we find a freestanding spot directly at the ocean in Deba.

Parking lot in Deba
N-634, Deba (Park4Night)
43°18'02.8" N, 2°20'41.9" W

Until we reach Bilbao, we are always oriented to the coast and, as a result, end up traveling on small country roads. Our parking spot in Bilbao is located above the city, which at first we look down on only from above in the dark.

Parking spot above Bilbao
124a Kobeta, Bilbao
43°15'35.6" N, 2°57'50.2" W

The next day we comfortably take the bus directly into the center of the city. First, we go to the Mercado de la Ribiera, which is the largest covered market in Europe at about 2.5 acres (10,000 m²). Fruit, vegetables, meat, fish, and many homemade items are sold here, and a bar area with many pintxos is also there. Later, we explore the old city and make our way to the Plaza Nueva, a gigantic square with many restaurants. Strolling along the river, we can't miss the opportunity to visit the Guggenheim Museum. Modern and contemporary art is shown here, and the building already catches your eye from the outside with its various sculptures.

We take the camper the next day to the actual landmark of the city—the swaying Vizcaya Bridge. It is the oldest transporter bridge in the world and is still in use today. The actual ferry hangs below the steel construction and swings over the river on long steel cables.

Gijón is famous for its *sidra* (cider), so we set out in the city in search of it. We are strolling through the alleys when an older lady speaks to us. She was born in Gijón and spontaneously takes us to her favorite restaurant, Los Espumeros. Of course, we order a bottle of cider and watch the waiter as he pours our drink. He holds the bottle with his right hand high above his head and has the glass in his left hand, far below.

Above: The famous spider of the Guggenheim Museum in Bilbao
Below: Drive through the Bardenas Reales badlands

The sidra is foamed at this height into the glass, and the sip is drunk immediately, so there is still a lot of air in the drink. That's why you never get a full glass, just a sip.

Sidreria Los Espumeros de Cimavilla
Calle Rosario, 56, Gijón
Open Tuesday through Sunday
from 12:00 p.m. to midnight
43°32′48.3″ N, 5°39′53.3″ W

In the late afternoon we drive toward the west and sleep in Atalaia Camper Park.

Atalaia Camper Park
Lugar Forxan, 2E, Lugo (Park4Night)
Phone: +34 982 188 494,
www.atalaiacamperpark.com
43°34′45.3″ N, 7°16′25.6″ W

Low tide is at 9:35 a.m., two hours before we reach the Praia das Catedrais. This way, we have about four hours to look at the arches, cliffs, and caves before the ocean takes back the beach. We park our camper quickly in the parking lot, which is also used as a free-standing location, and go down the steps to the beach. The sun is rising and shines on us through the arch of the approximately 100-foot (30 m) cliff, while the impressive nature is mirrored in the puddles. The roaring sea

to one side, the cliffs to the other. We are so fascinated that we completely forget about the time and just make it back before the tide comes in.

Praia das Catedrais or
Praia de Augas Santas
Praia das Catedrais, Ribadeo,
Lugo (Park4Night)
Parking spot 43°33′10.5″ N, 7°09′25.5″ W

Back at the camper, a small delivery van drives out front, opens its back doors, and becomes a small bakery. Perfect timing; we are about to starve.

To finish everything off, we still want to go to Ourense because the city is full of hot springs, and we are ready for a nice, warm bath. We find a freestanding spot quickly, and from there it is not far to the public pool or a closed bathhouse. We decide on the bathhouse because of the showers. The pool temperatures vary from comfortably warm to really hot. It is simply wonderful!

Freestanding spot near Ourense,
close to the springs
8 Paseo do Tinteiro, Ourense (Park4Night)
Parking spot 42°20′58.5″ N, 7°52′45.2″ W

Above: Sculpture made from the bottles of the famous *sidra* of Gijón
Below: Praia des Catedrais in the early morning at low tide

In the next chapter, we drive all the way through Portugal, but here we will continue with Spain's southern coast.

Coming from Portugal, we visit the western Spanish town of El Rocío. The streets are sandy paths: the horsepower here doesn't come from machines but from four legs. A really cool place, and Steffi as western and horse fan is in seventh heaven.

We are familiar with Seville already and love it. Now, in January, the temperature is also very comfortable. Since we prefer parking spots with surveillance systems in big cities, we drive to the Área Autocaravanas Sevilla. Not a very idyllic spot, and the showers are—especially for the men—pretty disgusting, but the spot is secure and watched twenty-four hours a day.

Área Autocaravanas Sevilla
Av. Garcia Morato, Sevilla
Phone: +34 619 26 13 25, p
sevilla@areasautocaravanas.com
Parking spot 37°21'46.0" N, 5°59'40.1" W

In Seville, we dedicate ourselves to everything having to do with the flamenco. We start our tour at the Plaza de España, an impressive square with a diameter of 650 feet (200 m), and also where a band with a dancer is performing flamenco. In the neighboring Maria Luisa Park, we discover the small green parrots. In the center we visit the Giralda, which was built as a mosque but later transformed into a church. The cathedral next to it is simply gigantic and similarly nice to look at. In Sevilla there is also a large tapas culture, and we enjoy the bite-sized delicacies in the Bar Estrella, of course with a *tinto de verano* to go with it—sparkling red wine.

Tapas bar Estrella
Calle Estrella, 3, Sevilla
Phone: +34 954 21 93 25,
www.barestrellasevilla.com
Open daily from 12:00 p.m. to midnight
37°23'18.4" N, 5°59'29.3" W

From the Metropol Parasol we look over the city as the sun sets—beautiful! A flamenco show in the Museo del Baile Flamenco is the crowning end to the day. The liveliness and strength that radiate from the flamenco dancers are indescribable. First class.

Now, we travel from the big city to the small white village of Vejer de la Frontera. In Andalucia there are many of these white villages. Vejer de la Frontera lies on the top of a hill: the streets are narrow, the houses glow white in the sun, and the many flowers provide a beautiful contrast.

Top left: The white village of Frigiliana in Andalucia
Middle left: Mule-drawn carriages in the western town of El Rocío
Top right: Western backdrop in the Tabernas Desert
Below: Sunset on the Metropol Parasol in Seville

A very bumpy trail leads to our spot for the night, but our campervan managed it well, and we are rewarded with a terrific spot on the ocean (prohibited today).

Alternate parking in Barbate
Calle Galeón, Barbate
+34 606 92 82 10,
www.areacañosdemeca.com
36°11'17.0" N, 6°01'19.2" W

During the winter, the otherwise so lively Tarifa is pretty tranquil. It is the quintessential windsurfing hotspot, with sandy beaches that go on almost forever. The sand partially accumulates into high dunes, and at Puna Paloma, a street goes over the large dune. With good visibility, you can see Morocco. A terrific spot, and of course we also find a freestanding spot directly on the beach—unfortunately, a sign was put up since then, prohibiting overnight stays.

As we leave Tarifa a few days later, two white villages, Casares and Mijas Pueblo, lie right on our route. Casares is especially beautiful due to its unique location embedded in a hill. Mijas Pueblo is unfortunately already very touristy, and we highly discourage anyone from using the donkey transportation.

The destination for today is Málaga. We have been in this city—if you combine all our past visits—for a total of almost a whole year, so we know our way around and start the day with the best churros in Café Aranda. Afterward, we stroll through the Mercado Central, simply because it is so nice to look at everything offered. We spend the rest of the morning in the old city, stroll through the streets, and pass the Basílica de la Encarnación and the Teatro Romano. Around midday we eat a few tapas in the old city, and in the afternoon we climb up to Alcazaba and look over half of Málaga and the harbor. We go back down on the harbor side and also stroll through the Jardines de Puerta Oscura park before we enjoy the traditionally sweet Málaga wine in Antigua Casa de Guardia.

We then prefer to spend the rest of the afternoon at the beach in the Pedregalejo neighborhood. There are also bars and restaurants there for dinner. If we want something a little more local, than we just walk farther east to El Palo. This is where fish is the order of the day: for example, *espetos*—sardines on skewers—are a specialty here. And our absolute insider tip for hungry party animals is the El Pimpi Florida in El Palo. Of course, we don't do all of that in one day: we have a lot of time. But those are some ways a perfect day in Málaga could be spent.

Above: The barrels at Antigua Casa de Guardia store Malaga's sweet wines.
Below: Churros and *pitufo con tomate* make up the best breakfast in Málaga.

Freestanding spot, Málaga
Calle Miguel de Merida Nicolich, Málaga
(Park4Night)
36°41'05.6" N, 4°27'35.4" W

Restaurant Iberico, Mesón las Hazuelas
Calle Encarnación, 9, Antequera
Phone: +34 952 70 45 82,
www.mesonlashazuelas.es
Open daily from 1:00 p.m. to 3:00 p.m. and
from 8:00 p.m. to midnight
37°01'00.3" N, 4°33'29.3" W

After so much time in the city, we are drawn back to nature. El Torcal lies in the backcountry—a natural park with beautiful hiking trails among massive rock formations. Even in the summertime, it is somewhat cooler here. For dinner, we are back in Antequera and eat delicious tapas in Mesón las Hazuelas. In addition, there is a free place to park in Antequera.

Área Autocaravanas Antequera
Av. Miguel de Cervantes, 43,
Antequera (Park4Night)
37°01'16.8" N, 4°34'18.1" W

A last white village lies on our route, so we drive to Frigiliana, another beautiful village with whitewashed homes, decorative flowers, and well-maintained streets. But this village

is also no longer a hidden gem. The drive to Almería leads through endless "plastic deserts" of greenhouses. The plastic sheets stretch to the ocean, and we became conscious for the first time where the cheap vegetables in the supermarket come from. Even the entry to the Cabo de Gata Natural Park leads through the "plastic desert" for quite a while. In the park itself, there is nothing to be seen of the plastic. Wild landscapes, hills, and beautiful sandy beach coves are a mark of this part of Spain. We spend the night at the Cabo de Gata Motorhome Area, a well-maintained spot, but still in the middle of the plastic jungle.

Cabo de Gata Motorhome Area
Carrerera Cabo de Gata, San Jose, Km 15,100,
Almería
Phone: +34 673 82 18 88,
info@cabogatacamper.com
Open all year
36°48'59.3" N, 2°08'57.4" W

Our last stop in the south is the Tabernas Desert, the only desert in Europe. It's well known as a film location, and its multiple western cities attract visitors. We want to drive out into the desert but don't find any suitable roads.

Spain is unbelievably diverse, impressive, and full of culture. Now we have also traveled it in our campervan as a first, and it was an absolutely fantastic time.

Above: Lonely beaches at Cabo de Gata
Below: We see many mountain goats in El Torcal Natural Park.

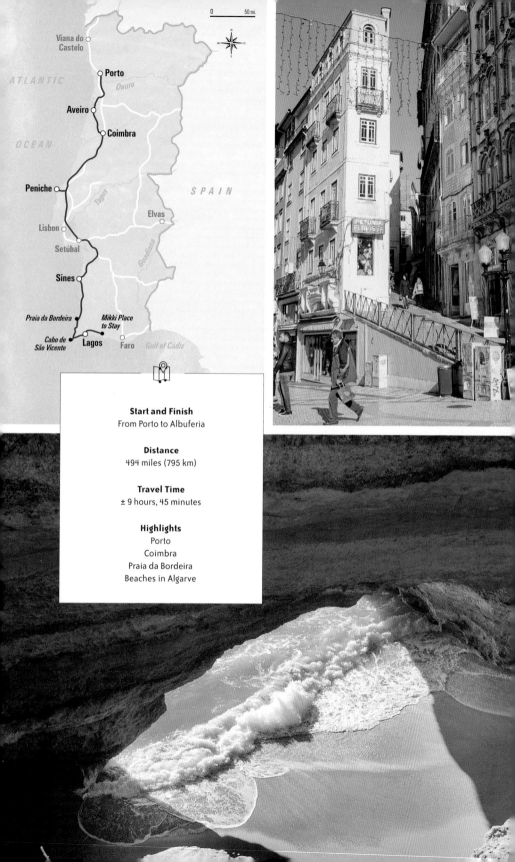

Viana do Castelo

Porto

Douro

Aveiro

Coimbra

ATLANTIC

OCEAN

Peniche

Tagus

SPAIN

Elvas

Lisbon

Setúbal

Guadiana

Sines

Praia da Bordeira

Mikki Place to Stay

Cabo de São Vicente   Lagos   Faro   *Gulf of Cádiz*

0   50 mi.

Start and Finish
From Porto to Albuferia

Distance
494 miles (795 km)

Travel Time
± 9 hours, 45 minutes

Highlights
Porto
Coimbra
Praia da Bordeira
Beaches in Algarve

Portugal

THROUGH PORTO AND COIMBRA TO THE BEST PLACE FOR SNOWBIRDS:
THE ALGARVE

We spend the winter in Portugal—although the route, of course, can be driven during different times of the year. We enter the country in the north and first pay a visit to Porto.

Once we arrive in the city center, we explore the indoor market of Mercado do Bolhão. Along with groceries, specialties, flowers, and souvenirs are also offered. Right next to it in the Manteigaria confectionery, the famous *pastéis de nata* are freshly prepared, and we are even able to watch. We treat ourselves to two of the delicious egg custard tarts and watch the colorful hustle and bustle outside through large windows. Afterward, we stroll through the alleys and pass Livrario Lello bookshop. A never-ending line of people are waiting to enter, because this is where J. K. Rowling got her inspiration for the Harry Potter books, and yes, the stairs do have a certain similarity to scenes from the films. For us, however, the nearby church Igreja do Carmo is much more exciting,

especially from the outside. Its facade is decorated with hundreds of small *azulejos*—colorful tiles—which together form one large picture. These pictures made from the regional tiles can also be seen in the Porto São Bento train station. From there we go toward the river and pass the Porto Cathedral, where we get a terrific view over the city from its terraces. We continue a little farther and stand on the Ponte Dom Luís I, the metro bridge. From up here we can see the neighborhood of Ribeira with its colorful homes and the port wine ships on the Douro. We go down there next. Ribeira has a unique flair—many bars and restaurants invite you to sit and stay. We sit down in the Bacalhau restaurant and drink a glass of port wine while we wait for our food. We slept a little outside the city at Camping Parque Campismo Salguerios. A simple and inexpensive campground, and the bus that runs directly to the city center stops right at its entrance.

Above: The old city of Coimbra
Below: The Benagil Cave in the Algarve region from above

Camping Parque Campismo Salgueiros
R. Campismo 263, Porto
Phone: +351 227 718 230, geral@canidelo.net
Open all year
41°07'15.4" N, 8°39'39.8" W

A few days later, we continue to Aveiro, which is known for its colorful boats in the city canals. These immediately catch our eye as we explore the city. We stroll a little through the alleys, but Aveiro doesn't really put us under its spell. We like the adjacent Ria de Aveiro lagoon as well as the headland with the Praia de Costa Nova much better—the colorful houses especially impressed us. The parking spot at Praia da Vagueira is also located on this headland, where we slept during a heavy storm.

**Parking spot Parque de campismo
da Praia da Vagueira**
Rua do Labrego, Praia da Vagueira
Phone: +351 969 098 598,
www.vagasplash.com/autocaravanas/
Open all year
40°32'58.3" N, 8°46'15.8" W

The next city on our route is Coimbra. For this, we drive a little into the backcountry and park our campervan at Parque do Choupalinho. We reach the old city over the Pedro-e-Inês Bridge, where we go directly to the visitor center at the entrance to the pedestrian zone and take a city map with us. We let ourselves be led through the streets and land in front of the Igreja de Santa Cruz church. We look at it from the inside too and view the beautiful gardens. We want to go from the lower old city to the upper old city, so we pass through the Torre de Almedina. We hear music coming from a store, *fado*, the soul of Portugal. In Coimbra there is a variant of it, called *fado de Coimbra*. If you want to listen to a concert with *fado* music, there is one daily at 6 p.m. in Fado ao Centro, which is right behind the Torre de Almedina. In the upper old city, we notice the Old Cathedral of Coimbra (Sé Velha), which looks more like a castle. Coimbra is a university city, with the campus located high up, where we go through the entrance. You can view various locations, including the massive library, which is worth seeing. And when we see a few students in the traditional robes, we are reminded of the Hogwarts school uniform. J. K. Rowling also took some inspiration from here. On the way back in the pedestrian zone, we pass by the Pastelaria Briosa Coimbra and buy ourselves the specialty: *briosa*, a strudel pastry, filled with a very sweet almond cream.

In the evening we meet up with friends on the free parking spot on the Costa de Lavos and spend a nice night together.

Above: Freestanding spot in the Algarve region, with a view of the ocean
Below: The traditional colorful boats of Aveiro

Parking spot Costa de Lavos
12–14 Rua Mestre Cardoso, Costa de Lavos
40°05'16.3" N, 8°52'31.9" W

Portugal is known as a surfer's paradise, and the waves are especially high in Nazaré because of the reefs off the coast. The Big Wave Contest takes place here every year, but you can find surfers in the water here year-round. We watch them from the Farol da Nazaré lighthouse and stroll through the small town a little afterward. Our next stop is in Peniche, but we can't view the cliffs and the old city because it's continuously pouring down rain. The forecast isn't giving us any good news either, so we continue on until we see the sun again and land around 230 miles (370 km) south, at the Praia da Bordeira.

A river passes the parking lot to the ocean, and it separates us from the massive landscape of sand dunes, which stretch to the ocean. We take the foot trail along the river and come to the cliffs, and from there we can cross the river and end up standing in the dunes. A captivating spectacle of nature—we stay here a few days and soak up the sun.

But at some point, we feel like we must continue. On the way to Cabo de São Vicente, we pass the Praia da Cordoama. It's another very impressive beach, surrounded by steep coastal cliffs. We get the best view of the coast somewhat north of Miradouro do Castelejo.

Freestanding spot, Praia da Bordeira
Estrada da Praia (overnight stays prohibited)
37°11′33.8″ N, 8°54′08.9″ W

The whole coast is full of such small beaches, and there would be countless ones to explore, but we drive farther to Cabo de São Vicente. The cape is the most southwestern point of the European mainland, and here you can eat the "last sausage before America" at a food stand.

Afterward, we drive to the fortress parking lot in Sagres to spend the night and are able to enjoy a uniquely beautiful sunset over the Praia do Tonel (overnight parking prohibited since 2021).

Alternate parking: Parque de Campismo Orbitur
Cerro das Moitas, Sagres
+351 282 624 371, www.orbitur.pt
37°01′28.3″ N, 8°56′46.7″ W

We still want to look at Lagos. We find a parking lot across from the Mercado Municipal, on the side of the road, and stroll through the indoor market first thing. Then we explore the alleys, stroll the old city, and discover a green-tiled house on the Praça Luís de Camões. Somewhat outside the city is the Ponta da Piedade, a place where turquoise water meets the rocky coast, and various caves and arches have formed.

At Camping Mikki's Place to Stay we bunkered down for a whole month. The campground is Dutch run and offers complete infrastructure in an informal setting. In addition, the Portuguese police normally start giving warnings and tickets to freestanding campers in January, because the supposed freestanding paradise of Portugal actually has laws that prohibit precisely this behavior.

Camping Mikki's Place to Stay
Areias de Pera 700A, Pera
Phone: +351 913 70 03 02,
info.mikki.f@gmail.com
Open all year
37°07′43.5″ N, 8°19′22.8″ W

In the following weeks we still do excursions and explore the coast, which invites us with its sensational cliffs and beaches. Praia de Benagil, Marinha, Albandeira, and Morena are a few of the many sights worth seeing. And then comes the time to leave Portugal. We continue to Spain (see the tour through southern Spain in the previous chapter) and are happy to be back on the road.

Previous double page: Praia da Bordeira, with a terrific freestanding spot right next to it
Above: Lighthouse at Cabo de São Vicente
Below: Terrific sunset in Sagres—freestanding spot right next to it

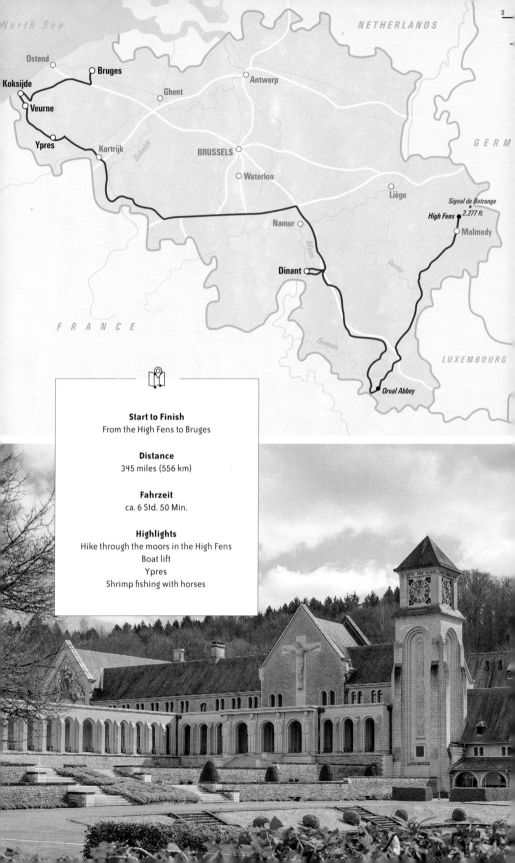

North Sea

NETHERLANDS

0

GERM

Ostend

Bruges

Koksijde

Veurne

Ypres

Kortrijk

Ghent

Antwerp

Scheldt

BRUSSELS

Waterloo

Liège

Signal de Botrange
High Fens ● 2,277 ft.

Malmedy

Namur

Maas

Durthe

GERMANY

Dinant

Orval Abbey

LUXEMBOURG

Semois

FRANCE

Start to Finish
From the High Fens to Bruges

Distance
345 miles (556 km)

Fahrzeit
ca. 6 Std. 50 Min.

Highlights
Hike through the moors in the High Fens
Boat lift
Ypres
Shrimp fishing with horses

Belgium

MOOR LANDSCAPES, TERRIFIC TOWNS, AND CRAB FISHING HIGH ON HORSEBACK

We don't have high expectations when it comes to Belgium, since no one has ever raved to us about it before. We picked out a few destinations, and then we will continue on—that's our plan. But plans can change, which turns out to be the case at our first destination: the High Fens Nature Park and Fagne Wallonne. We park the campervan at Maison du Parc-Botrange in Waimes and start the Noir Flohaj hike, which leads us about 8 miles (13 km) through nature. Soon after we begin, we can see the massive moor landscape. First, we walk across the ground, but later, when the ground gets too wet, jetties lead through the moor. A captivating landscape, it is just emerging from its winter slumber.

Near the dam Barrage de la Gileppe, there are a few free parking spots for campers, including electric hookups. We spend the night there and look down at the dam from the restaurant Lac de la Gileppe.

Barrage de la Gileppe parking spot
Route de la Gileppe 55a, Jalhay (Park4Night)
50°35'15.5" N, 5°58'11.1" E

The Circuit de Spa-Francorchamps racetrack is not much farther, so we drive there and watch a few hobby drivers run their laps.

Shortly before the border with France, we reach our next destination, the Orval Abbey. It is a monastery of an order of Trappist Cistercian monks that—as is commonly done in Belgium—owns its own brewery and cheese dairy. We explore the grounds, look at the buildings and the garden, and of course taste the beer.

From the Orval Abbey we drive a little more than an hour to Dinant. The little city on the Maas stands out not only because of its beautiful houses and the accompanying old city worth seeing, but also the impressive, centuries-old citadel high on the rock behind the city. We spend the night in its parking lot under the trees.

The Orval Abbey—beer is also brewed here.

Apparently, there is now a sign prohibiting overnight parking, but spending the night in the restaurant parking lot should still be allowed.

Parking lot at the restaurant near the Citadel
Chemin de la Citadelle 15, Dinant
50°15′40.1″ N, 4°54′59.0″ E

The next morning, we drive farther toward the sea. Along the way, we pass the gigantic Strépy-Thieu boat lift. It is a lift for cargo ships that raises and lowers the ships about 328 feet (100m) vertically in huge boxes filled with water. So, it has little to do with a classic lock system. There are even technical tours and boat trips through the lift. There are parking spots on both sides of the structure, where you can also spend the night. However, we continue—the weather is not good enough today to spend hours looking at ships. We ended up spending the night at a small marina directly on the water: we love spots like this.

Marina in Péruwelz parking spot
4 Rue Ponchau, Péruwelz (Park4Night)
50°31′07.1″ N, 3°36′33.1″ E

In Ypres, we catch a dry window to look at the city in West Flanders. At the Grote Markt we get a city map from the tourist information center, with a recommended city tour, and immediately marvel at the impressive, Gothic building complex of the Cloth Hall, known as Lakenhalle van Ieper in Flemish. The belfry extends up from the building, a 230-foot-high (70 m), narrow bell tower, which tolls beautiful music every thirty minutes. The Menenstraat leads us to Kasteelgracht, where we go up some steps to the old city walls. There is also a war memorial here, where a horn is played daily to remember the British soldiers. We choose to go back through the old city, past countless houses from the Middle Ages, and land at Ieperse Katjes. There are all different sorts of Belgian chocolate here, also in cat forms. And because we have seen so many symbols, logos, and now chocolate in the shape of a cat, we ask what it all means.

Ieperse Katjes— finest Belgian chocolate
Neermarkt 4, Ieper
50°51′02.8″ N, 2°53′06.2″ E

Above: Strépy-Thieu boat lift—in operation on the left
Below: Housefronts on the Grote Markt in Ypres

In the Cloth Hall there was a large infestation of mice, and the rodents ate the precious cloth. Cats were the perfect solution, until they reproduced so much that they became another plague themselves. The people did not know how else to fix the situation other than to catch the cats at the end of the winter and throw them from the belfry. There is still a festival to mark this event today, but of course only stuffed-animal cats have been thrown to the crowd for a long time.

After the city tour we drive on, and finally we reach the ocean! Our excitement doesn't last long, however, since the Belgian coast is very densely overbuilt. Even on the street N34, which runs right along the ocean, we can see some sand and water only once in a while among the tall buildings. We actually wanted to fall asleep to the sounds of the ocean, but we decide to look inland for a suitable place and find it in Veurne in a marina on the canal—and for free.

Marina Veurne parking spot
Kaaiplaats 2, Veurne (Park4Night)
51°04'12.3" N, 2°40'0.4" E

We have a good reason for staying in the region. The next day we drive to the public beach of Oostduinkerke in the early morning, and we soon hear a deep, leisurely *thump,*

thump, thump. We then see the gentle giants, softly pushing their large hooves on the asphalt. Horses, more precisely "cold-blooded" horses of the Belgian Brabanter breed, pull carts behind them until just before the sea. There they are resaddled; the coachmen climb up onto their powerful horses in the wooden saddle and wade out belly-deep into the sea.

Each end of the nets is attached to a horse and rider, and the powerful animals pull the nets parallel to the coast through the water. As the colossal horses leave the water after a stretch, the catch emerges: small shrimp! Afterward, they are cooked and sold on-site. We also get ourselves a bowl after the spectacle, and wow, they taste delicious and couldn't be any fresher! This old tradition of shrimp fishing with horses is done on predetermined days from April to September a few times a month.

Of course, Steffi is in on cloud nine after experiencing so much horsepower and can't seem to get her fingers away from the animals' damp coats. Lui really enjoys the eating part at the end—we both are thrilled by the experience.

Shrimp fishing with horses
Oostduinkerke Public Beach Zeedijk 442a, Koksijde
Dates and Times: www.visitkoksijde.be/de/die-krabbenfischer-zu-pferde
Finding parking is difficult, so plan some extra time.
51°07′59.5″ N, 2°40′16.7″ E

The ferry to Great Britain is booked, but we still don't want to miss Bruges. We park our camper on Professor-Dokter-J.-Sebrecht-Straat and go to the old city comfortably on foot. In the city center we explore the many small streets, marvel at the beautiful buildings from the Middle Ages, walk over the typical cobblestone roads, and stroll along the canals. Along the way we pass the Church of Our Lady, Boniface Bridge, the Quay of the Rosary, the 270-foot (83 m) Belfry of Bruges with its forty-seven bells, and the Market Square. Bruges is really a beautiful city worth visiting.

And so, our trip through Belgium ends much differently than we expected. We really like the small country and found many terrific cities, impressive landscapes, exciting traditions, and one commonality with Switzerland—the love of chocolate.

From Dunkirk, France, the ferry takes us to Great Britain—are you coming with us?

Previous double page: Out with the shrimp fishermen and their Brabant horses
Above: Eyeing the catch after the hard work
Below: View from the Boniface Bridge in Bruges

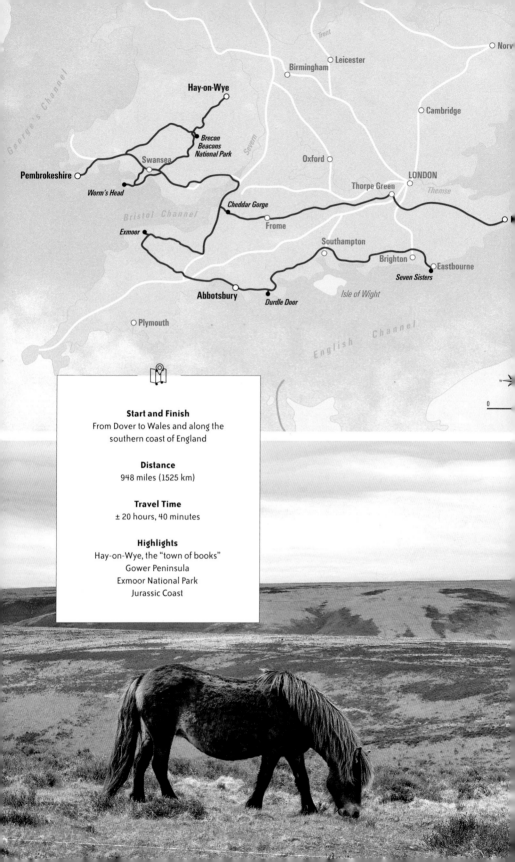

Norv

Leicester

Birmingham

Cambridge

Hay-on-Wye

Brecon
Beacons
National Park

Severn

Oxford

LONDON

Swansea

Thorpe Green

Themse

Pembrokeshire

Worm's Head

Cheddar Gorge

Bristol Channel

Frome

Exmoor

Southampton

Brighton

Eastbourne

Seven Sisters

Abbotsbury

Durdle Door

Isle of Wight

Plymouth

English Channel

0

Start and Finish
From Dover to Wales and along the
southern coast of England

Distance
948 miles (1525 km)

Travel Time
± 20 hours, 40 minutes

Highlights
Hay-on-Wye, the "town of books"
Gower Peninsula
Exmoor National Park
Jurassic Coast

Great Britain

TO A TOWN OF BOOKS, ALONG THE WELSH COAST, AND THROUGH SOUTHERN ENGLAND'S NATIONAL PARKS

After arriving in Dover, it is definitely an adjustment to drive on the left side of the road, with our steering wheel on the left side. Having an attentive passenger at some intersections is a big help. Much more difficult, however, are the speed limits in miles per hour. Mental math at every new speed limit sign? No, Steffi notated the speeds on our dashboard with erasable marker. Problem solved: now the journey to Bristol can begin.

We are not here because of the city, but because our first destinations are located close by. We spend the night in Bristol on the edge of a large park before we start our hike in the Cheddar Gorge the next day.

Freestanding spot, Bristol–Westbury Park
B4054, Parrys Ln, Bristol (Park4Night)
51°28'42.2" N, 2°37'08.9" W

The weather is typically English. It's drizzling, and fog is obscuring the view. Even in the visitor center at Cheddar Gorge we are discouraged from doing the hike on the rocks up the gorge—it's too slippery, and we wouldn't have any kind of view anyway. So, we are content with a drive among the high rocks and only a short hike on flatter terrain.

In Clevedon on the Bristol Channel, the sun is shining. We want to take advantage of it and explore the town on foot. There are typically British homes with manicured gardens, and on the coast there is a beautiful pier. If you want to go on it, you must pay a few pounds. We soak up the sun while eating an ice cream, then we drive to the moated Caerphilly Castle, by which we crossed the border to Wales. First, we stroll through the expansive park before we cross the bridge at the entry gate into the castle. There is currently a kite exhibition in the castle courtyard, and even the rooms inside the fortress can be viewed.

An Exmoor pony in Exmoor National Park

Along the way to Hay-on-Wye, we go shopping and find out that there is almost always a gas station at the large supermarkets and that there, the gas prices tend to be the lowest. For a liter of diesel, we pay 1.18 pounds (about 1.36 euros). Toward the evening we arrive in Hay-on-Wye and spend the night in a large parking lot at the edge of a field.

Hay-on-Wye parking spot
Offa's Dyke Path, Hay-on-Wye (Park4Night)
52°04'21.5" N, 3°07'31.2" W

Today we are going to Steffi's personal paradise: Hay-on-Wye is the first and still the largest town of books in the world! Whole houses are full of books from the basement to the attic. New books, old books, novels, nonfiction books, and historical books—a dream for every bookworm. There are over forty antiquarian bookshops, meaning bookshops that specialize in the sale of used books, and countless "normal" bookshops are in the town. Even in the alleys there are shelves full of books; in the tourist information center you can buy some, and in the cafés and even in the castle garden you can get books for a small donation. Good that we are not on the edge of the vehicle-weight capacity for our campervan, because Steffi easily brings about 10 pounds of books into the camper, beaming.

Let's get out of here, although the town admittedly is very beautiful.

The next day we go hiking in Brecon Beacons National Park. For this, we visit the visitor center of the national park and are advised there so nicely that we barely can leave again. Yes, the Brits are very open to travelers and like to chat. Since there is a lot of moor landscape in Brecon Beacons, a drier path is recommended to us. So, we hike over fields and trails to the Twyn-y-Gaer viewing point and take another path back to the camper. We arrive around midday at the Erwlon Caravan and Camping Park, so we have enough time to thoroughly test the washing machine.

Erwlon Caravan & Camping Park
Brecon Rd., Llandovery
Phone: +44 1550 72 10 21, www.erwlon.co.uk
Open all year
51°59'37.8" N, 3°46'55.1" W

Back at the ocean, today is dedicated to cliffs and beaches. We drive over the A4118 starting at Swansea out to the Gower Peninsula. The street is narrow—along the sides there are large hedges growing, and street crossings are difficult, even though Steffi has done well getting used to driving on the left. We make our first stop at Three Cliffs Bay.

Above: With the Irish Ferry you can reach Ireland from Wales.
Below: In a bookstore in Hay-on-Wye

We park at Three Cliffs Bay Holiday Park and go to the bay on foot. The first views down from above are terrific. A bay filled with sand, with a chain of rocks coming from the left to the ocean, at the end of which stand three striking cliffs: Three Cliffs Bay. We start the climb down and soon notice that the tide is coming in, because the bottoms of the cliffs are starting to get wet. Because we aren't looking for the same thing to happen to us, we turn back. There's more coming.

In Rhossili we park at Worm's Head, where we also spend the night. The view of the endless beach of Rhossili Bay is fantastic. We go along the cliffs on foot to the headland of Worm's Head. The English grass is mowed perfectly short along the way. The sheep and wild hares do their jobs well. It is said that sometimes seals can be seen here, but we didn't have any luck in that regard. But we treat ourselves to a delicious dinner of fresh fish and chips in Worm's Head Bar and Restaurant.

**Worm's Head parking spot
(overnight parking prohibited)**
Rhossili, Swansea (Park4Night)
51°34′09.0″ N, 4°17′21.0″ W

The next day, we drive along the coast to Pembrokeshire Coast National Park, and along the way we stop and circle around Carew Castle

on foot. After arriving in the national park, we take our first hike to Stackpole Head. For this, we park the campervan at the Boathouse Tearoom and follow the Pembrokeshire Coast Path westward. We make our way to Barafundle Beach down some stairs and go back up the cliffs at the end, until we reach Stackpole Head. Surrounded by the ocean on three sides, we see a small island just off the coast that is full of birds. At the next bay, we go back into the backcountry, follow the Fishpond Lake, and experience nature here from a totally different perspective.

Somewhat farther west at Freshwater West Beach, we find a parking area for the night (now prohibited) and sit until the sun has disappeared from on the beach and off the cliffs.

There are seaweed burgers with egg for breakfast from the ship snack car, Café Môle, in the large Freshwater West Beach parking lot. We spend the day here at the beach, and in the evening we drive to Pembroke Dock and take the ferry to Ireland from there.

Alternate parking: Newton Farm, Pembroke
Call Rowland: +44 777 04 304 86
www.newtonfarmcampsite.co.uk

Above: Algae burgers for breakfast at Freshwater West Beach
Below: Hike through Brecon Beacons National Park

The tour through Ireland is described in the next chapter—here we continue with our return to Great Britain two weeks later.

Back in Great Britain, we put some distance behind us and drive to Exmoor National Park. Exmoor is the home of the Exmoor ponies, and, of course, Steffi wants to see them. We follow the road A39, and starting at Porlock it goes up the hill at an incline of up to 25 percent. Along the road we discover the first half-wild Exmoor ponies. We follow the road to Lynton, where we spend the night at the Channel View Caravan and Camping Park.

Channel View Caravan & Camping Park
Manor Farm, Barbrook, Lynton
Manor Farm, Barbrook, Lynton
Phone: +44 1598 75 33 49,
www.channel-view.co.uk
Open from March 15 to November 15
51°13′05.0″ N, 3°49′45.8″ W

Today we take the even-smaller B3223, which is somewhat narrower, but the nature around us is even more special. Untouched land as far as the eye can see—here only the ponies are responsible for the landscape, and we see multiple herds. We even see a herd of deer on the side of the road and plenty of pheasant. Tarr Steps Woodland National Nature Reserve is only a little off the route, and because

it's Sunday, the Sunday roast is being served in the Tarr Farm Inn. We take our after-dinner walk along the Barle River, and later we visit the Exmoor Pony Center, where Steffi can also pet them now. Rides through the national park are also possible here.

In the late afternoon, we leave Exmoor and drive along the southern coast of England, which is called the Jurassic Coast here. We love the drive through Abbotsbury so much that we look for a place to spend the night and then explore the town and the surroundings on foot. It is so unbelievably beautiful here—the homes are very well maintained, and the flowers are blooming in all colors in the yards. We enjoy the evening mood from the ruins of St. Catherine's Chapel before we stroll back to our van.

Freestanding spot, Abbotsbury
3 Rodden Row, Abbotsbury,
Weymouth (Park4Night)
50°39′54.4″ N, 2°35′51.3″ W

We eat breakfast in Weymouth on the Isle of Portland on the southern point, near the lighthouse. Afterward, we also explore Chesil Beach, which is made up of almost fist-sized round pebbles, and the farther north you go, the smaller the round pebbles become.

Above: Through the alleys of the "town of books" Hay-on-Wye
Below: The pebbles of Chesil Beach on the Jurassic Coast

Before the age of technology, fishermen would be able to recognize their location along the beach on foggy days on the basis of the size of the pebbles.

The highlight for us along the Jurassic Coast is the Durdle Door. We park our car at the Durdle Door Car Park to see it and go by foot along the South West Coast Path toward the west. After only a few yards we discover the Man O'War Beach and then the Durdle Door arch in the turquoise-colored water. The sandy beaches are snow white, and with high limestone cliffs towering behind them, which in turn are overgrown with thick green grass. Along with the terrific blue shades of the ocean, it's simply beautiful.

After going a good bit farther east, we arrive at a farm in Eastbourne at sunset, where we spend a somewhat quiet night directly on the sheep pasture, since the sheep end up bleating the whole night.

Today is then also our last day in England already, which we spend once again on a hike along the cliffs. We are at the Seven Sisters in East Sussex, where we walk past the Beachy Head Lighthouse, which sits far below us in the water, to Birling Gap. The time has really come to try a cream tea there. What sounds like just a drink is actually a full meal: a scone with strawberry jam, clotted cream on top (boiled down, thick cream), and a tea to go along with it. There's only one thing to say about it: delicious! And then we are already driving kilometers (or, better said, miles) to Dover, where we can fortunately take the ferry in the evening twelve hours earlier thanks to the Flexi-Ticket from DFDS Seaways.

By the way: Great Britain counts as a country: Wales, England, and Scotland are only parts of it, which is why we left out Scotland and spent more time in southern England and Wales. We will surely visit Scotland sometime in the near future.

Parking spot at the Seven Sisters Farm
Beachy Head Road, Eastbourne (Park4Night)
50°45'14.4" N, 0°15'03.6" E

Above: The Durdle Door on the Jurassic Coast
Below: View of the Beachy Head Lighthouse

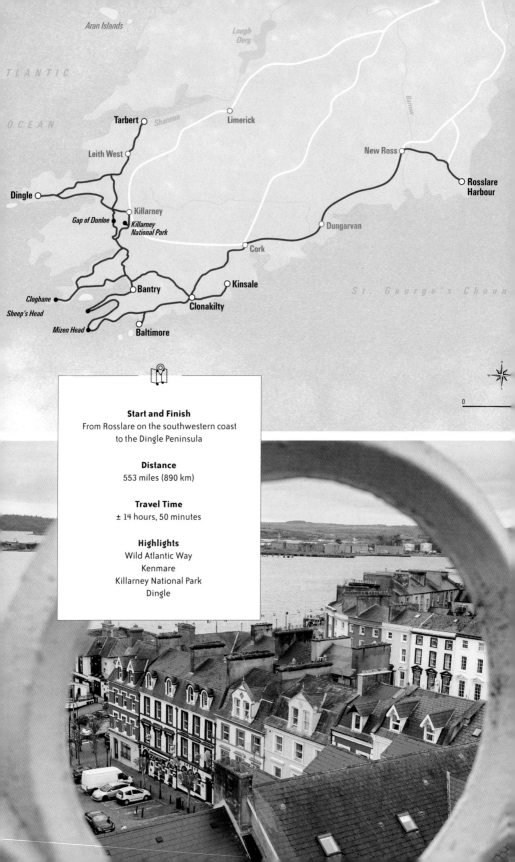

Aran Islands

Lough
Derg

TLANTIC

OCEAN

St. George's Chann

Tarbert ○ Shannon

Limerick ○

New Ross ○

Rosslare
Harbour ○

Leith West ○

Dingle ○

○ **Killarney**
Gap of Dunloe ●
Killarney
National Park

○ **Dungarvan**

○ **Cork**

○ **Kinsale**

Cloghane ●
Sheep's Head

● **Bantry**

Clonakilty

Mizen Head ●

○ **Baltimore**

Barrow

N
W — E
S

0 [_____]

Start and Finish
From Rosslare on the southwestern coast
to the Dingle Peninsula

Distance
553 miles (890 km)

Travel Time
± 14 hours, 50 minutes

Highlights
Wild Atlantic Way
Kenmare
Killarney National Park
Dingle

Ireland

QUIRKY TOWNS AND NATURE HIGHLIGHTS
ON THE SOUTHERN WILD ATLANTIC WAY

We arrive by ferry into Rosslare Harbour early in the morning and begin our exploration of the island in Cobh. The town used to be called Queenstown, which was the port town of the *Titanic* when it went down in history. Cobh presents itself well in a few areas, but if you look a little past it, there is not much else. We are not big fans, so we soon continue.

Today we find a place to spend the night on Inchydoney Beach. The tides show themselves in a spectacle of nature as they let us see a little more and then a little less of the beach.

Freestanding spot, Inchydoney Beach
Inchydoney Island, Clonakilty (Park4Night)
51°35′48.0″ N, 8°52′07.0″ W

After eating breakfast among the dunes, we explore the town of Clonakilty. We like it here much better. The colorful houses are better maintained, and on Ashe Street and Pearse Street we literally feel the life pulsating. In Richy's Restaurant and Café, we eat a traditional Irish breakfast—okay, it's more like a lunch in our sense. Eggs, ham, toast, sausage, and a slice of original Clonakilty black pudding, comparable to blood sausage. Lui likes this specialty so much that we buy some black pudding sausage for ourselves on the way back at Edward Twomey Butchers.

The Wild Atlantic Way is calling: a 1,600-mile (2,600 km) sightseeing route along the western coast of Ireland. Starting in Clonakilty, we follow the brown signs, which lead us directly along the coast. Long Beach on the R598 impresses us—we stand on the black cliffs for a long time and look out at the waves of the turquoise-colored water. We drive around the Mizen Peninsula and the Sheep's Head headland completely, both small, lesser-known routes, which include the whole spectrum of the Wild Atlantic Way: rugged rocky coasts, wild landscapes, colorful fishing villages.

The colorful old city of Cobh is not just beautiful.

Hungry Hill Camping Site
Adrigole Harbour, Adrigole
Phone: +353 831 196 659,
info@hungryhilllodgeandcampsite.com
Open all year
51°41'37.9" N, 9°43'30.8" W

The streets, however, are very narrow. We are often very happy that we have a van and not anything wider. At the end of an unbelievably great day, we finally check into Hungry Hill Camping Site.

Here in Adrigole Harbour, seals can often be seen sunning themselves. We end up also being able to see them a little later from the shore. Today we are going to dedicate ourselves to the Beara Ring, the little sister of the famous Kerry Ring. We marvel over the fantastic, wild nature, and the colorful villages such as Eyeries, and we enjoy the grand views along the way. Somewhere on the side of the road in a pull-off, we can't pull ourselves away from the amazing view, so Steffi runs into the campervan and ten minutes later we are eating lunch with this view. Traveling in a camper is simply amazing! At the end of the Beara Ring, we arrive in Kenmare and fall shockingly in love! A small town with a pulsating street full of life, the colorful homes decorated with the typical Irish script. And it's to be expected that there are more pubs

than hairdressers. We also go in one and are overcome by the charming interior, including a fire in the hearth.

Because we are pressed for time, we must decide between the Kerry Ring and the Dingle Peninsula, and we end up choosing the latter. So, we take the N71 through Killarney National Park, another route worth seeing, which often leads through moor landscapes and forested regions. Shortly before reaching Killarney, we hike to the Torc Waterfall. On a knoll behind the forest, we find a nice freestanding spot with a view of the Lough Leane lake.

Forest parking lot near Killarney
Turn right in Gortagullane Upper
(Park4Night)
52°00'56.5" N, 9°28'47.9" W

The next morning, we circle this lake and drive up to the Gap of Dunloe. The journey ends for all vehicles wider than 7'2" (2.2 m) at the bridges. We just made it through with a vehicle width of 6'7" (2 m). Carriages drive along here starting around midday, so we tried to be there early. The nature is indescribably beautiful and gloriously wild—we could simply look at the landscapes here forever.

Above: The cliffs near Long Beach on the Wild Atlantic Way
Below: Pubs in Kenmare—we also end up in one.

The Dingle Peninsula is also wonderfully beautiful. The weather unfortunately was not very kind to us, so we don't get to see too much of the terrific views. We really like Dingle itself as well. The small town captivates you with its many beautiful houses and small shops. We enjoy Dingle so much that we spend the night in the harbor and let the evening come to an end in Foxy John's Pub and Hardware Store (yes, actually two in one).

Parking lot in Dingle Harbour
Dingle Harbour, R559, Dingle (Park4Night)
52°08'20.9" N, 10°16'37.4" W

Along the R560, we finish the route around the Dingle Peninsula—the part around the Connor Pass is especially beautiful. We drive up to Tarbert—starting in Tralee, we don't find the area particularly worth seeing and turn around. The section of the N71 between Kenmare and Bantry has once again a terrific pass road, and the street is wide enough for you to really enjoy the views.

We spend the night in Ballydehob at a channel that is full to the top at high tide— even a seal swims inside—and at low tide a path across the channel emerges.

Soon the time comes to journey back to Rosslare. Ten days have passed, and our booked ferry is waiting. Ireland deeply touched our hearts—the landscapes and the people are simply terrific. It even appears on the list of countries for us in which we could imagine living.

Freestanding spot at the channel at Ballydehob
2–12 Store Rd, Ballydehob (Park4Night)
51°33'39.4" N, 9°27'25.6" W

Above: Hike on the N71 near Derrycunihy Church
Below: Thanks to driving on the left side, Steffi can pet the Irish horses at the wheel.

Start and Finish
From Middelburg to Utrecht

Distance
156 miles (252 km)

Travel Time
± 4 hours

Highlights
Middelburg
Zierikzee
Tulip blooms in Lisse

Netherlands

ISLAND HOPPING WITH THE CAMPER
AND FORAYS THROUGH THE TULIP FIELDS

Coming from Belgium, we travel directly into the province of Zeeland—one of the most beautiful regions of the Netherlands. We take the tunnel in Terneuzen and already have ended up on the peninsula of Walcheren. Middelburg is the capital of the province, where we find ourselves at a live concert in a bar the first night. The next day, there is a market in the main square in front of the Stadhuis, one of the most significant Gothic buildings in the Netherlands. We generally really like the buildings, but Lui finds the town so great that he sticks an "I Love Middelburg" sticker on our campervan!

In Domburg, we want to go to the beach. In the village, however, the parking spots cost 2.20 euros per hour—they are free a little farther out. The white sandy beach stretches endlessly in both directions: a few mobile homes stand below—now that would be something! We eat the smoked mackerel from the market in Middelburg and enjoy the terrific weather at the water.

Our loose cash continues to be in high demand—parking lot near the tourist information center, parking fee at the Oranjezon Nature Reserve, including an entry fee. It all comes together to be quite a sum at the end of the day. Half-wild horses and fallow deer live in the nature reserve. It is also beautiful at the beach of Vrouwenpolder, especially at the Aloha Beach Bar, which is located right in front of the nature reserve.

Parking spot at Roompot Beach Resort
Kamperland (Park4Night)
51°35'22.6" N, 3°42'59.4" E

In the Netherlands, spending the night in the open (freestanding) is not allowed, which is why we drive to the Roompot Beach Resort, which also offers a place to park.

Today is not just any day, but Koningsdag (King's Day), where you see a lot of traditional orange clothing, parties, and free markets, because on Koningsdag you don't need a license to sell goods on the street. We start the day in Zierikzee at a flea market with a live band and nicely decorated streets.

Above: Signpost at the North Sea
Below: Koningsdag in Zierikzee—everything is nicely decorated.

At the Oude Haven we notice the very pretty townhouses, all of which slope forward at the top. The reason for this is the rope hoists on the roof gables that were used in the past.

On the N57 we hop from one island to the next until we arrive on the mainland near Rotterdam. Even there, celebrations are being held in every quarter, live bands are playing, and people are drinking beer. The buildings along the different channels are also very beautiful once again. Here we dive into the masses as well in the different parties and markets, and the city spits us back out in the evening.

The best part about small countries is that we can simply drive to our next destination in the evening and spend the night there. So, we drive to Lisse, where the only legal free-standing spot was located, but it is prohibited today. Many campers are nestled among the colorful tulip fields at a dead end.

Alternate Parking: Camping Sollasi
Duinschooten 14, Noordwijkerhout
+31 252 37 64 37, www.sollasi.nl
52°17'04.8" N, 4°30'19"

Around Lisse, it is very easy to find tulip fields. The tulip fields stretch, for example, endlessly along the Leidsevaart Channel. We take a few arching routes around Lisse and continually discover new fields and colors. If you also want to see the full blooms in meticulously planted beds and like to have a lot of people around, you can visit the Keukenhof, but one look at the full parking lot was enough for us.

It takes us a long time to find a parking spot in Utrecht. On the Oudegracht—old channel—we stroll into the center of the city, past even-more-beautiful buildings from the Middle Ages. In the city center, there is a lot going on, and at every corner you can find the Dutch favorite, French fries, with countless sauce options. You can also find cheese dairies, and of course tulip bulbs are being sold. Yes, Utrecht gives our tour through the Netherlands a crowning finish.

On our way south, we spend the night for the last time in the country. To Lui's delight, we found another beautiful parking spot at a marina at Camperplaats de Punt.

Camperplaats de Punt parking spot
De Punt, Gorinchem (Park4Night)
51°49'36.7" N, 4°57'52.8" E

Top left: Cheese wheels at the market in Middelburg
Top right: Tulip fields near Lisse
Below: Channels and bicycles—two things in Utrecht that can't be missing

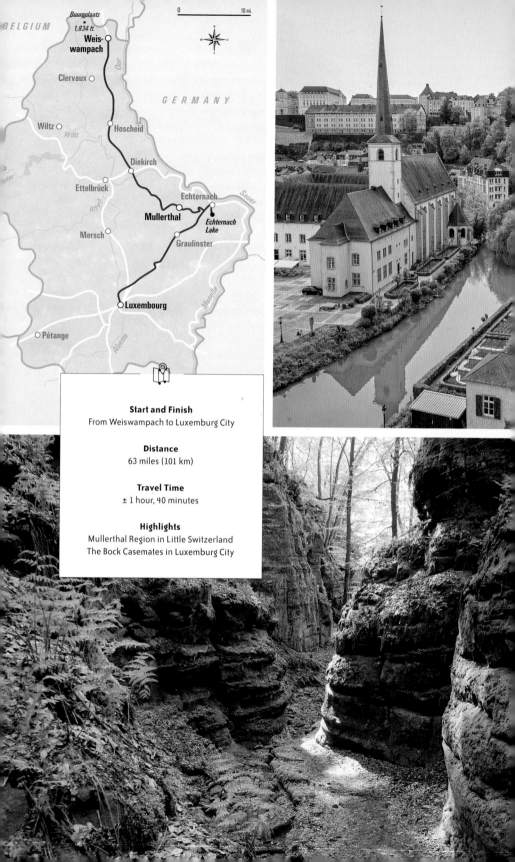

Start and Finish
From Weiswampach to Luxemburg City

Distance
63 miles (101 km)

Travel Time
± 1 hour, 40 minutes

Highlights
Mullerthal Region in Little Switzerland
The Bock Casemates in Luxemburg City

Buurgplaatz
1,834 ft.

BELGIUM

Weis-
wampach

Clervaux

GERMANY

Wiltz

Hoscheid

Diekirch

Ettelbrück

Echternach

Mullerthal

Echternach
Lake

Mersch

Graulinster

Luxembourg

Pétange

Luxembourg

CASTLES, HIKING IN LITTLE SWITZERLAND, AND A VISIT TO THE CAPITAL

Our thirty-third country is Luxembourg, and we don't travel it alone but are guided by our blogger friends Tascha and Patrick, a.k.a. *Patascha's World*, through their home country. Our meeting point is far in the north, and again we arrive with our gas tank showing a deep red because everyone knows that gas is especially inexpensive in Luxemburg, and we also find out that it's the same price at every station in the country.

We soon leave Weiswampach behind us, drive toward the south, and pass by Vianden Castle. On road 322 there is a viewing point (49°55′56.3″ N, 6°12′06.2″ E) from which we look upon the complete castle grounds.

Of course, the two bloggers lead us into Little Switzerland, better known as the Mullerthal Region. Starting in Bergdorf, we follow the B2 trail and hike through the forest, through gorges, among rocks, and even through a robber's den (*raiberhiehl* in the local language). Back at our campervan at the Hammhafferstroos, we are soon sitting at the communal grilling spot and feast at the joint barbeque. In Mullerthal, we spend the night in a paved parking lot (prohibited today).

Alternate parking: Camping Park Beaufort
Grand-Rue 87, Beaufort
+352 83 60 99 300,
www.campingpark-beaufort.lu
49°50′22.7″ N, 6°17′20.5″ E

We drink our first coffee where we spent the night, and then we continue to Echternach Lake. There we eat an abundant breakfast on the wooden platform and watch the wild turtles that live in the lake. Afterward, we drive to Luxembourg City, where the vans park at Parking du Glacis. We stroll along Parc Kinnekswiss into the city center and soon stand at the edge of a gorge. There are two gorges that run through the capital, with the Adolphe Bridge being the most unusual—a double-decked stone arch bridge that has had its own path for pedestrians and bicyclists since 2017.

Above: View from the Bock Casements to the old city of Luxembourg City
Below: Hike to the Raiberhiehl in Mullerthal
Following double page: Castle Vianden from the described viewing point

In the old city, we also come across the statue of the former grand duchess and the Grand Ducal Palace, which is still occupied.

At a Pilgrim's Market we order two traditional specialties: *gromperekichelcher* (potato pancakes) and *choucroute* (roll with sausage and sauerkraut).

We get a terrific view of the old city from the Bock Casements—this underground tunnel complex was previously an air-raid shelter and can still be viewed today. And then it was finally time to say *Äddi*—goodbye in Luxembourgish!

Skagerrak

Skagen
Rubjerg Knude Lighthouse
Frederikshavn
Løkken
Læsø
Hanstholm
Fjerritslev
Kattegat
Heltborg
altring
Viborg
Randers
Ringkøbing Fjord
Aarhus
Samsø
Fredericia
Zealand
Esbjerg
Kolding
Ribe
Funen
Rømø

30 mi.

Start and Finish
From Rømø to Skagen

Distance
327 miles (527 km)

Travel Time
± 7 hours, 50 minutes

Highlights
Ribe
Tversted Naturlegeplads
Råbjerg Mile
Skagen

Denmark

ALONG THE COAST, INCLUDING SAND DUNES AND
LIGHTHOUSES TO THE NORTHERN POINT

Our tour of Scandinavia starts in Denmark. First, we visit Rømø, an island just off the shore, which is accessible over a dam. At Lakolk, you can also drive on the beach with campers, but you aren't allowed to stay the night. In Denmark, free camping is illegal, but spending the night in your vehicle, as in so many countries, is a gray area. We wouldn't have a problem outside the regular season in well-chosen spots; however, we would like to expressly point out that each person bears his own responsibility for this.

We arrive in Ribe in the late afternoon. We park in the city's own parking lot and go by foot into the center. The path there already leads past beautiful homes—flowers are blooming everywhere, and everything is well maintained. We just manage to catch the daily tour that starts at 8 p.m. with the night watchman at Torvet, and explore the oldest town in Denmark. We really like Ribe, and even after the tour we stroll leisurely through the streets.

Freestanding spot in the center of Ribe
Stampemøllevej 1, Ribe
55°19′28.7″ N, 8°45′27.5″ E

In the parking lot in Ribe, we are parked literally door to door with other campers, which is why we drive to the beach at Skallingen in the early morning and park at the end of the Skallingevej street. The beach runs farther than the eye can see in both directions. We leave the beach in the afternoon and want to eat the famous cake from the Farm Café in Nørre Nebe. Unfortunately, the café is completely full, so we continue on without the cake.

Near Ringkøbing we find a beautiful freestanding spot at a fjord, where we spend the night (prohibited today).

Above: Typical specialty platter in Café Slugten in Lønstrup
Below: Through Ribe with the night watchman

Alternate parking: Stellplatz Ringkøbing
Fiskerstræde 60, Ringkøbing
56°05'10.6" N, 8°14'26.5" E

The next day is supposed to be really hot, so we want to go to the beach of Fjaltring and make our way there. You used to be able to spend the night here, but when we visited there was a sign forbidding it. So, we just go swimming and enjoy the day here. At the camper parking lot in Handbjerg, we get a spot and spend the night once again in a marina.

We found this spot with the app DACF– Danish Camper Association, where many official parking spots and farms are noted.

Handbjerg camper lot
Handbjerg Marina 12, Vinderup
56°28'47.4" N, 8°43'05.1" E

Thy National Park lies before us—it is the oldest national park in Denmark. Along with many birds, large deer populations live here—even otters feel at home. We want to start a hike from the Isbjerg parking lot, but it's raining and storming. We spend the night, hoping for better weather, and in the morning a herd of cows walks by, but they don't bring the good weather with them. So, we continue.

**Isbjerg freestanding spot,
Thy National Park**
Hindingvej 45, Thisted
57°02'27.3" N, 8°36'59.6" E

However, there are people enjoying the windy days. In Hanstholm, we observe kite- and windsurfers that have met their match. We go to the beach ourselves and then head to Løkken. At the pier, you can also drive on the beach, but we get stuck in the sand even earlier, because it's storming here as well, and there are some sand drifts that are so deep that our camper gets stuck. We let the wheels rotate until they have dug through to the asphalt, and we escape, but we don't want to hear any more about driving on the beach today.

We found the campground with a farm flair in Løkken on the DACF app as well. We ride out the storm here and notice for the first time how much longer the days are up here in the north.

Above: A beautiful residential area in Ribe
Below: The Rubjerg Knude lighthouse on a drifting dune
Following double page: Out and about on the huge Råbjerg Mile migrating coastal dune

Café Slugten
Strandvejen 96, Lønstrup
Phone: +45 98 96 06 33, www.cafeslugten.dk
Open daily in the summer from 11:30 a.m. to
10:00 p.m.
57°28'22.1" N, 9°47'50.7" E

Camping Parking Løkken
Løkkensvej, Løkken
57°23'22.6" N, 9°46'27.6" E

Sunshine and blue skies—the nice weather is back, and we use it to explore the Rubjerg Knude, a lighthouse on a migrating coastal dune. And because the dune upon which the lighthouse sits is slowly moving inland, it's probable that within the next few years, the earth under its base will break away, and it will collapse into the ocean.

Lønstrup is the next town to the north, and there we eat at Café Slugton. We order a fish platter and can try multiple regional Danish specialties.

Afterward we stroll through the cute town until we reach Lønstrup Klint, the beach, and follow the coast over the dunes. The path leads us in an arc back to the center of the town, where we get back into our campervan and drive to Tversted Naturlegeplads. We park the camper in the parking lot for the night, but we still hike through the forest until we reach the ocean and later grill at the large grilling spot and playground. It is an idyllic place.

We are getting close to the northernmost point of Denmark, but on the way there we make another stop at the Råbjerg Mile, a massive dune landscape that moves about 50 feet (15 m) west each year. It came from the North Sea and is projected to disappear completely into the Baltic Sea in the year 2160.

This sandy landscape covers an area of about 300 acres (120 hectares), and we scramble around somewhere in between, climb the dune ridges, and have a fantastic view all the way to the sea.

Tversted Naturlegeplads freestanding spot
Tranevej, Bindslev
57°36′10.1″ N, 10°14′12.9″ E

And then the time comes to visit Skagen. First, we stroll through the northernmost town in Denmark—the streets are very full, though, because there are two cruise ships that are anchored here today. We drive a little farther north and go on foot for the last stretch to the northernmost point at the beach of Grenen. Sometimes seals are said to lie on the beach, but they have long since disappeared during today's rush. At the very tip, we see it with our own eyes—the waves approach from both the right and the left. This is where the North Sea and the Baltic Sea meet, or, more precisely, the sea regions of Skagerrak and Kattegat. Another day it would have certainly been a once-in-a-lifetime experience, but since it is filled with hundreds of people today, it is difficult to feel any deep emotions. But it was still very impressive for us to see.

At sunset, we are already on the ferry on our way to Sweden. Denmark was a positive surprise for us. We had already been in the country before with a car and a tent, but we never really warmed up to it. But now on this tour, we discovered really exciting and beautiful places and landscapes. And there is also available infrastructure for traveling with a camper, even if freestanding camping is forbidden and highly controlled during peak travel seasons.

POLCIRKELN
Napapiiri
Arctic Circle
Cercle Polaire
Polarkreis

Start and Finish
From Göteborg (Gothenburg) to Gustavsfors and
from Östersund into Abisko National Park

Distance
859 miles (1,382 km)

Travel Time
± 18 hours, 40 minutes

Highlights
Archipelago of Gothenburg
Glaskogen Nature Reserve
Trollforsen
Ajtte Museum in Jokkmokk
Abisko National Park

Sweden

A CAMPER'S DREAM IN GLASKOGEN NATURE RESERVE AND THROUGH THE SWEDISH LAPLAND

We arrive by ferry in Göteborg in the middle of the night and immediately drive out of the city to Stensjön lake to spend the night. In the district of Haga we meet Steffi's friend. It is a hip district with vintage stores and nice cafés where you can buy fresh cinnamon buns. We enjoy the botanical garden south of Haga, in which the children's zoo is nestled where Sweden's wild animals live in large enclosures. On the way back, we stroll along the Kungsportavenyn, one of the main streets with stores and cafes. In the Feskekörka on the other side of the channel, you don't pray to fish, which you might infer from the name meaning "fish church," but they are sold in the market hall and in the restaurants. In a somewhat different way, the treasures of the sea sure are revered here.

We repark our van to a somewhat more central location and spend a few nights at the Liseberg Camperarea Skatås—not at the campground, but in the parking lot somewhat above it.

Liseberg Camperarea Skatås parking spot
Skatåsvägen 25, Göteborg
Phone: +46 31 84 02 00
Open from May 1 to November 3
57°42'10.3" N, 12°02'07.3" E

We first can explore one of the highlights of the Göteborg area upon leaving the city— the Archipelago of Göteborg. We choose our route in such a way that we drive along the coast on the main roads and through Tjörn and Orust. The views of the rugged coastline and archipelago islands are terrific. We arrive at Lake Väner in the early evening and discover an amazing freestanding spot at the edge of the woods. We quickly make a fire and soon are in the mood to grill. Surrounded by woods on the banks of the lake and all alone, without even mosquitos—yes, this is what makes van life fun.

Above: Crossing the sixty-sixth parallel—the Arctic Circle in Sweden
Below: Spectacular Trollforsen Rapids at Lake Övre Trollselet
Following double page: Now looking back at the Tjörnbron Bridge after crossing

Freestanding spot at Lake Väner
5 Slottet, Mellerud (Park4Night)
58°36'12.1" N, 12°36'06.4" E

Parking lot in Karlstad
11 Treffenbergsvägen, Karlstad (Park4Night)
59°22'18.0" N, 13°29'21.0" E

The FIFA World Cup had begun, and Lui had picked out a sports bar in Karlstad. So, we continue along Lake Väner and watch the game that evening. We spent the night in an official and free camper lot in Karlstad.

We have picked out a few nice routes from our street atlas for today. We follow road 62 north and are soon surrounded by forest. And there, an elk hops off the road over a guardrail and disappears into the forest. Our first elk in the wild.

We turn left in Ekshärad onto road 239, another nice route, and we continue driving through terrific landscapes spotted with the typical red-and-white houses. A little farther and we have arrived in Glaskogen Nature Reserve and find a heavenly freestanding spot. We launch our canoe, make a fire, and grill out for dinner. We first discover weeks later that free camping is forbidden throughout the natural park, which is why we won't reveal its location and instead suggest using Glaskogen Camping in Glava.

For us, it's laundry day once again, and we enjoy our stay at Vammervikens Camping so much that we extend our stay for a few more nights. Apparently, an albino elk has been living in the area for years, but on our extensive walks we don't even see a brown one. But the hikes were beautiful anyway.

Vammervikens Camping
Vammerviken, Väg 172, Gustavsfors
Phone: + 46 531 201 07,
info@vammervikenscamping.se
Open from May 15 to September 15
59°13′22.3″ N, 12°07′52.0″ E

We continue after a few days, and after only a few miles we already cross the border to Norway. We go on an impressive tour through the south and come back into Switzerland farther north. We will continue here with this second chapter—the journey through Norway will be in the next section.

Back in Sweden we drive on the E45 via Östersund, which now brings us through the Swedish Lapland. We still want to see the midnight sun, so we have to keep going.

The detour to Lake Övre Trollselet, with its spectacular rapids, is something we aren't going to miss, so we drive a good 10 miles (15 km) over bumpy roads to reach the lake, where we also spend the night. A hiking trail leads us from the banks of the lake to the rapids of the tributary. The landscape with the wild river embedded in it is incredibly beautiful.

Freestanding spot, Lake Övre Trollselet
Unnamed road, Moskosel
66°01'28.5" N, 19°16'22.3" E

The next day, we reach the magical sixty-sixth parallel—the Arctic Circle. Up here, the sun shines at midnight on the longest day of the year. If you're driving on the E45, you can't miss the large sign. Lui wants a certificate as a souvenir and gets one in the visitor center somewhat beyond the parking lot.

Jokkmokk lies a little farther north, where we visit the Sami Museum of Ajtte. Using an informational brochure, we explore the rooms and learn a lot about the Sami, the Indigenous people of Lapland, as well as the flora and fauna, of course including the reindeer. We keep seeing them more frequently on the roads. We stop the first time and take a picture; then, on repeat occasions, we merely drive carefully to make sure that they don't run in front of the campervan.

We go on a hike far in the south of Muddus National Park, where the Lule River has turned into a lake because of a huge dam built there. There is a well-maintained path that starts at the visitor center and goes through the forest, which is currently full of ripe berries, and leads to another river. That evening, we spend the night on the bank of the lake and even jump in.

Freestanding spot at Muddus National Park, clearing by the lake
Leave the E45 after the dam, go under the road, and drive a few miles.
66°47'00.1" N, 19°59'17.0" E

Above: A different kind of traffic in the Swedish Lapland: reindeers
Below: Out and about in Abisko National Park

The next day, we go to Kiruna. We don't especially enjoy the northernmost city in Sweden, with its large ore mine, which is why we continue to Abisko National Park, where, shortly before reaching it, we find a green parking lot to spend the night. The mountains are somewhat in the way, but around midnight we still see the rays of sun peeking behind the clouds. It was really something special!

Freestanding spot outside
Abisko National Park
Parking lot on the E10 shortly before Abisko
68°20′49.0″ N, 18°56′59.3″ E

First, we look around the next morning in the visitor center at Abisko National Park. Afterward, we start our walk into the heath, through the birch forests, and trudge bravely through the impressive high moor. The well-known Kungsleden long-distance hiking trail also runs along here.

Back at the campervan, we drive to the ICA supermarket for the last time, buy a few dear grocery items, and leave Sweden once again toward Norway.

Swedish dream: Freestanding spot with a hammock in Glaskogen Nature Reserve

120 mi.

Nordkapp

Hammerfest   Kirkenes

Tromsø

Senja

Norwegian   Narvik   Riksgränsen

Sea   Bodø

SWEDEN

FIN-
LAND

Trondheim
Hjelsetveien   Kopperå
esund   Geirangerfjord
igardsbreen

Bjørgavegen

OSLO

*Baltic
Sea*

auda   Nomeland

avanger

orth Sea

Start and Finish
From Nomeland to Trondheim and from Narvik
to the North Cape

Distance
1,407 miles (2,264 km)

Travel Time
± 1 day, 18 hours, 25 minutes

Highlights
Suleskarvegen
Stavanger
Hjelmelandsvågen
Snøvegen
Nigardsbreen Glacier
Gamle Strynefjellsvegen
Senja Island
Fishing on the North Cape

Rytmefeber
presenterer
Call me ♪
Betty

Norway

BREATHTAKING PASS ROADS AND HIGH IN THE NORTH:
THE ALTERNATIVE TO LOFOTEN TO THE NORTH CAPE

Above all, we are looking forward to the amazing nature in Norway, which is why we pass by Oslo and find ourselves on the highest mountain road in southwestern Norway a few hours later. The Suleskarvegen runs along between Nomeland and Lysebotn. We drive to the Lysefjord past snowfields, summits, and mountain lakes and are amazed over and over again by the fascinating landscape.

In Stavanger, we spend the night in a residential parking lot, which is pleasantly quiet despite the street next to it.

Freestanding spot, Stavanger
50 Tjodolvs gate, Stavanger (Park4Night)
58°57'32.9" N, 5°43'23.3" E

Stavanger itself is a straightforward town—we explore the city center and the old city, where we especially enjoy the Øvre Holmegate street with its colorful wooden homes. At the old harbor, we have something to drink and let the evening come to an end.

The next morning, we take the ferry across to Tay, deliberately skipping Preikestolen and taking road 13 instead, which is marked as a route worth seeing. We follow it, enjoy the view along the fjords, and end up arriving in Hjelmelandsvågen, where we spend the night in a small harbor.

Hjelmelandsvågen parking spot
Fv644 9, Hjelmeland (Park4Night)
59°14'14.6" N, 6°10'44.9" E

We take the ferry to Nesvik, make a few turns, and end up on the breathtaking Birkelandsvegen mountain road, marked as road 520. The route leads through an impressive landscape for miles. We find our way back to civilization when we reach Håra, and past Låtefossen (*fossen* means waterfall) the road leads to Odda, where we find a parking spot on the lake shortly before reaching Tokheim.

Above: Midnight sun on Senja
Below: Øvre Holmegate street with its colorful wooden homes in Stavanger

Parking spot before Tokheim
Fv550 121, Odda
60°04′46.7″ N, 6°31′43.9″ E

We leave out Trolltunga after a short investigation reveals that the parking lot for the famous rocky outcrop costs sixty-two euros. Which is incredible, considering that Norway offers so many other impressive landscapes for free. Our highlight today is Snøvegen, or, in English, Snow Road. On the way there, we stop in Gudvangen and in Flåm and enjoy the views of the Nærøyfjord and the Auerlandsfjord. In the second fjord, a cruise ship is just leaving the harbor, and from up here it looks more like a small toy boat amid the gigantic mountains.

Shortly before reaching the Lærdal Tunnel, we turn off and drive up the steep, narrow side street. We are happy that we are driving up in the evening and there are hardly any cars coming in the other direction. From the Stegastein viewing point, we look down to the Auerlandsfjord, which is surrounded by the mountains. Words cannot express what we see—it's just so beautiful. And then we come to the high mountains. There is still some snow, and there are many lakes and a

barren rocky landscape. It is unbelievably pretty. Somewhere in the middle, we cook ourselves some dinner, which we enjoy outside in the unique nature. We are simply at a loss for words and deeply grateful that we can experience all of this.

Shortly before reaching Lærdalsøyri, we spend the night on the banks of the Lærdalfjords, a branch of the Sognefjords: the longest and deepest fjord in Europe.

Freestanding spot at Lærdalfjord
Fv243, Lærdal (Park4Night)
61°06′12.6″ N, 7°25′54.7″ E

At breakfast, we are once again on the ferry—most of the time, each ride costs between ten and fifteen euros. The tolls for the highways, tunnels, and other special roads are first due after the trip. On the website www.vegvesen.no, you can look at the toll prices, but, unfortunately, the page is only in Norwegian. In the menu on the top right, you must select "Bomstasjoner," and then a click on the different routes reveals the prices.

On the way to Nigardsbreen, we especially enjoy the route that starts in Gaupne, where road 604 leads along the Jostedøla River.

Above: Driving on the Suleskarvegen mountain road
Below: Piece of ice fished out of the river at Nigadsbreen

From the turquoise color of the water, we can pretty much assume how cold the water must be. From our parking spot, the view of the Nigardsbreen Glacier is fantastic—the turquoise-colored lake, the boulders, and the blue-white glacier behind it. The path to it leads over rocks and boulders—the hiking shoes were a good idea today despite the warm temperatures. The last climb over slippery, smoothed stones leads past the glacial river, which carries pieces of ice along with it. Steffi fishes a fist-sized piece out of it, and we both marvel at how crystal clear the ice is. We go very close to the glacier and touch it. With every approaching step, the temperature sinks. It's dripping and cracking all around, which makes sense on a sunny day around 77°F (25°C). A wonderful experience.

We drive a little farther north—then it's time to sleep again, even though it never gets any darker than sunset.

Freestanding spot on the river
E39, north of Klakegg (Park4Night)
61°38'16.5" N, 6°31'20.9" E

Today, the drive takes us to the next mountain road. Of course, we first take the ferry before we drive to Videsæter. There, we take a right just before we reach the tunnel entrance, which is where Route 258 begins as well as the Gamle Strynefjellsvegen. After a steep climb, the paved road turns into a single-lane gravel path. To our right, there is a bright, turquoise-colored lake, and in front of us the gray road and the mountains, with green patches between them here and there. The sun is high in the sky, without a cloud in sight. It's amazing how a landscape can touch you—once again, it is indescribably beautiful. A cold lunch platter is quickly prepared: a lunch in the most perfect place in the world.

At Langvatnet lake we drive toward Dalsnibba and Geirangerfjord. We avoid the tolls at the Dalsnibba viewpoint and drive directly to the fjord. After a few windy roads and a lot of traffic, we have arrived at Flydalsjuvet Rock. An overfilled parking lot alerts us to these rocks with a viewing spot. Yeah, okay, the view of the Geirangerfjord is spectacular—the cruise ship in it really puts the size of this landscape into perspective. However, the hustle and bustle in the parking lot and the traffic that was there only show us very clearly that we love the small, fine pass roads, like the Gamle Strynefjellsvegen we were just on, much more.

Above: The Nigardsbreen is an impressive glacier.
Below: Route 258 gravel road: the Gamle Strynefjellsvegen

We continue after arriving at the Geirangerfjord below, and once again we must go back up along the side over very windy roads. We feel a little sorry for our campervan. But the Opel Movano masters them well, and the many viewing platforms give the tortured engine lots of breaks.

Oh yes, the next ferry ride awaits us. So, let's go—everyone on board and over to Linge. The street on the other side leads us back into the much-loved mountains. We spend the night in the parking lot of the Trollstigen Center.

Freestanding spot on the Atlantic Road
Flatsetveien, Averøy (Park4Night)
63°02′20.2″ N, 7°32′56.0″ E

We are disappointed the next morning when we find out that the next part that we saw on Google Maps was not a further bridge road, but rather a tunnel, which will cost us fifteen euros in tolls. The actual Atlantic Road route is only a little over 4 miles long (7 km) and can be easily reached from Vevang, but afterward we would turn around and drive along the Kvernesfjorden to Bergsøya.

We drive around Trondheim and are now on our way back to Sweden, where we want to put the next 600 miles (1,000 km) behind us. Shortly before the border, we find another really beautiful freestanding spot with a rowboat that can be used.

Freestanding spot at Trollstigen Center
Trollstigen 1, Åndalsnes (Park4Night)
62°27′11.2″ N, 7°39′48.6″ E

In the morning, we take another hike before we drive down the troll steps—known as *Trollstigen*—ourselves. There is traffic in front of us because of travel buses, and once it dissolves, we also keep driving, past the three-headed troll statue and now headed toward the ocean.

The Atlantic Road is our last destination in southern Norway. Just one ferry and a few hours later, we reach the southern end of the Atlanterhavsveien at Vevang. Now there are bridges that lead us from island to island. We wait to start the second part, because we found an idyllic freestanding spot and spend the night directly at the ocean.

Freestanding spot on the Atlantic Road
E14, Meråker (Park4Night)
63°21′22.9″ N, 11°59′44.0″ E

Above: The famous Atlantic Road, or, in Norwegian, *Atlanterhavsveien*
Below: A beach north of Skaland made of pieces of coral

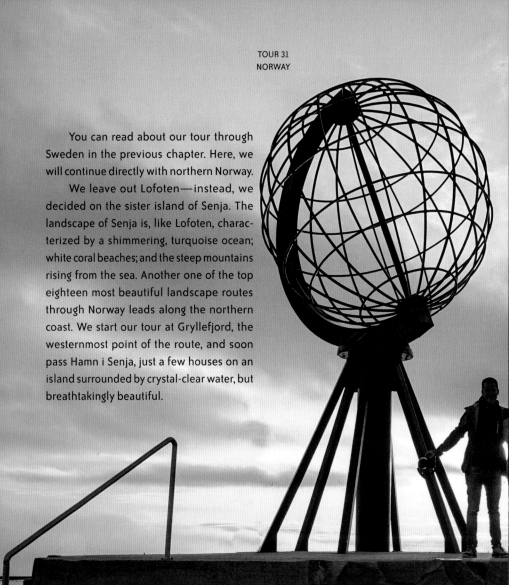

You can read about our tour through Sweden in the previous chapter. Here, we will continue directly with northern Norway.

We leave out Lofoten—instead, we decided on the sister island of Senja. The landscape of Senja is, like Lofoten, characterized by a shimmering, turquoise ocean; white coral beaches; and the steep mountains rising from the sea. Another one of the top eighteen most beautiful landscape routes through Norway leads along the northern coast. We start our tour at Gryllefjord, the westernmost point of the route, and soon pass Hamn i Senja, just a few houses on an island surrounded by crystal-clear water, but breathtakingly beautiful.

We pass the Bergsbotn viewing platform a little farther on and look out at the heavenly landscape. The blue fjord, the mountain massif, and the soft-green slopes are simply wonderful. We drive by Skaland until the road comes to an end. There is a white sandy beach above, which is covered with small coral pieces. Yes, I know we are repeating ourselves, but this place, too, is unbelievably beautiful.

At the Tungenset rest stop, we climb over the rocks to reach the headland. From here, we have the perfect view of the Devil's Teeth, a rugged chain of rocks with very sharp peaks.

Freestanding spot in Ersfjord
Fv 862, Skaland (Park4Night)
69°28'43.7" N, 17°23'40.0" E

We can also see the Devil's Teeth from the spot where we spend the night. And here, on a day that really couldn't have been more perfect, we experience the midnight sun for the first time.

The rest of the route to Botnhamn is also worth seeing, which is where we take the ferry again and even see porpoises along the way.

By the time we arrive in Brensholmen, it has officially been decided: we are driving to the North Cape. We still have around 500 miles (800 km) to go, which is why we decide to drive in a timelier manner. The sun shines twenty-four hours a day anyway, which is still something special. Somewhere along the way, we park in a parking lot around one in the morning and sleep for a few hours.

Along the way we see more and more reindeer—at one point we even see three at a time standing in the ocean, cooling themselves off. Even in the north, the summer of 2018 is a very hot one. There are small shops that sell reindeer fur and antlers along the way. Fish are dried on wooden frames as well. The landscape becomes increasingly barren: there aren't any more trees, and even the bushes are getting smaller.

We meet up with acquaintances from Switzerland in Honningsvåg, and the man plays us a song with the Swedish alphorn before we put the last miles behind us. Shortly after midnight, we arrive at the visitor center of the North Cape. The small parking garage is already closed, but the visitor center is still open. Shortly before 2 a.m., we are alone, the fog lifts for a moment, and we are standing at the famous globe in the sunshine. Yes, driving up here was worth it.

We stay a few days in the area somewhat south of the North Cape, pull two splendid salmon out of the water with the fishing rod, and simply enjoy life. Norway really showed us how privileged we are to be able to experience this fantastic journey. We give the country, despite the many tolls, a solid ten stars.

Previous double page: Sunshine at 2 a.m. at the North Cape
Above: Even reindeer need to cool off.
Below: In the north, stockfish are dried on large wooden frames.

0   30 mi.

NORWAY
Lake Inari
Inari
Ivalo
RUSSIA
Pallastunturi
Kemijärvi
Rovaniemi
Oulanka
National Park
Kemijoki
Kuusamo
SWEDEN
Kemi
Oulu
Lake Oulu
Siikalatva
Kajaani
Vaasa
Kuopio
Linnansaari
National Park
Varkaus
Särkisalmi
Mikkeli
Pori
Tampere
Saimaa
Turku
Kouvola
Helsinki
Gulf of Finland
Gulf of Bothnia

Start and Finish
From Lake Inari to Helsinki

Distance
1,194 miles (1,921 km)

Travel Time
± 1 day, 3 hours

Highlights
Pallas Yllästunturi National Park
Oulanka National Park with the Bear's Trail
Linnansaari National Park
Many solitary lakes

Finland

THROUGH LAPLAND, ON THE BEAR'S TRAIL, AND SEARCHING FOR SEALS

Coming from Norway, we make our way toward Lake Inari. Shortly before reaching it, we get ourselves some tips about the Finnish Lapland in a tourist center, as well as a fishing license, which for lakes can be conveniently found online at www.eraluvat.fi. We don't find Inari itself to be too special, so we quickly drive out into nature. There, the density of the reindeer populations quickly increases.

We don't want to follow the E75 but take the back road 955, starting at inari, which consists mostly of well-maintained gravel roads. This way, we pass through massive, people-free forests, moors, and what feels like hundreds of reindeer. Somewhere at the end of this route we also find a place to spend the night.

In Pallas Yllästunturi National Park, we start a hike at the visitor center up to the Palkaskeronkierros viewing point. It is not high, but Finland is so flat that this hill is enough to look over what feels like half the country. And along with forest, we see, above all, lakes! There are about 188,000 of them in the whole country, and we find a new one every evening that we tend to we have to ourselves.

Like today, for example, where we spend the night on the banks of Lake Pallasjärvi and add another day because we want to paddle out with the canoe, go fishing, and pick blueberries in the woods later—only the sauna isn't especially attractive on a day over 77°F (25°C).

Freestanding spot on Lake Pallasjärvi
Gravel road starting at Taloniemi (Park4Night)
68°00'06.7" N, 24°11'40.3" E

We like Finland right away. The landscape is not as spectacular as Norway with its mountains and fjords, but these many lakes and forests full of blueberries also have their charm.

Above: Licorice ice cream in Helsinki
Below: One of the many freestanding spots along a lake in Finland

At Camping Nilimella, we once again do all our cleaning, washing, and gray water (dirty water from the campervan dishwasher) disposal. Especially here in northern Finland, there are few places to dispose of gray water, so we readily use the campground.

Camping Nilimella
Kelukoskentie 5, Sodankylä
Phone: +358 16 61 21 81, info@nilimella.fi
Open from June 1 to September 30
67°25'02.9" N, 26°36'28.6" E

And what is something that most people never think of at the end of July in summer temperatures? Christmas! But whom are we going to visit now? Santa Claus! Will he be wearing shorts and a tank top? After arriving in Rovaniemi, we aren't going to miss the Christmas village. Many buildings belong to it, including Santa Claus's post office, where you can drop off letters all year long, but they will reach Santa only at Christmastime. A long corridor that puts you in the Christmas mood leads you to him. And yes, there he sits. Does he actually wear light, summer clothes? We don't want to destroy any fantasies—you must come here and see for yourself. The border to the Arctic Circle is also here in the village. But we are not yet ready to pass this magical border back into the south. So, we drive more or less exactly along the sixty-sixth latitude border. We want to hike in Oulanka National Park, but first we spend the night in full daylight on another beautiful lake. And from it we are even able to catch two perch: a delicious dinner is secured.

Freestanding spot near
Oulanka National Park
Sallantie 50, Käylä
66°17'35.8" N, 29°08'36.3" E

Today, we go hiking in Oulanka National Park, and we decide to undertake the Bear Trail. The starting point is at the visitor center in Juuma, where there is also informational material available. We pass through the forest, on jetties over the moors, and on suspension bridges to reach the opposite banks of the rivers. Thanks to the hot and dry summer, there are hardly any mosquitos—we also don't see any bears, but a few reindeer instead.

The drive continues to the south, and now we cross the Arctic Circle. We find our spot on the lake for the night at Kesi-Kero, but the fish won't bite.

Above: Out and about in Pallas Yllästunturi National Park
Below: Hiking on the Little Bear Trail in Oulanka National Park

Freestanding spot on Lake Keski Kero
78 Kerontie, Kuusamo
65°41′27.4″ N, 29°18′03.2″ E

We like the spots along the Finnish lakes so much that we now hop from lake to lake and spend the days either along the banks or paddling in the canoe. In order to do that, you have to be fully independent, because there isn't any infrastructure at the locations. After many nights, we are drawn to the ocean. We drive to Oulu and spend the day at the beach of Nallikari.

In the late afternoon, it's once again time for a ferry ride, and we go over to the island of Hailuoto, and because the ferry is part of the official road network of Finland, it's free. The small island is straightforward—after a few hundred yards we find a parking opportunity in a cove, where we spend the night at the water.

Freestanding spot in Hailuoto
Potinhamina 16, Hailuoto
65°03′33.6″ N, 24°53′07.3″ E

Today we explore the island and drive to the other end in Marjaniemi. There are campers in the harbor, with even some infrastructure available, but our place was definitely more beautiful. Next to it is a long

beach, and in town there is a small café as well as a restaurant with a buffet—the most common type of food service in Finland.

Back on the mainland, we park our camper on a headland near Raahe and spend another night at the ocean. There are a few mosquitos here, but nothing too bad.

For two weeks, we drive from lake to lake, finding beautiful new spots to park next to either a boat access spot or other small parking lots. We are not allowed to make any campfires due to the prolonged dryness, but it's too warm for that anyway.

Freestanding spot near Raahe
Pirttiniemi 36, Raahe
64°40′27.4″ N, 24°26′12.9″ E

In Linnansaari National Park and, with it, in the Finnish Lake District, we unpack the canoe once again and start paddling. This is where the Saimaa ringed seal is supposed to live, a rare species. We paddle the whole day among the islands but end up seeing only their leavings on a rock in the lake. The landscape is absolutely worth seeing, and the day on the water was wonderful.

On the banks of Lake Honkasensalmi, which is where we were already out and about during the day on our canoe, we find a nice little spot for our camper and enjoy the evening hours in the open.

Above: View from Palkaskeronkierros in Pallas Yllästunturi Nationalpark
Below: Searching for seals in Linnansaari National Park

Today, we look at the nearby city of Savonlinna. There is currently a flea market, so we stroll along the market stands. We see a few seals here, but we should probably also mention that these ones are cast in bronze.

Freestanding spot on Lake Honkasensalmi
On the canal of Tappuvirrantie 513,
Savonlinna
62°05′33.6″ N, 28°39′16.9″ E

Our mothers come to visit us in Helsinki for Steffi's birthday, which is why we drive back to the capital city a little more quickly. We still stop in Lahti, the famous ski town, and look around. We have rented an apartment in Helsinki because our campervan is much too small to accommodate four people.

Helsinki has multiple market halls, and we look around in the Hakaniemen Kaupaahalli and visit the outdoor harbor market, where we encounter the reindeer skins from Lapland once again and stroll through the Vanha Kauppahalli next door. There are many stands where you can try reindeer or elk meat, but there are only two varieties: either dried or in a burger. Outside at the ice cream parlor, we discover the typical licorice ice cream. As we turn up our nose at it, Steffi's mom goes ahead and orders the black ice cream and relishes it eagerly while we stroll through Esplandadi Park and listen to the street musicians.

We take the boat out to the island of Soumenlinna, which is a UNESCO World Heritage Site. It used to be a fortress compound made up of multiple islands, but today the military has made space for visitors, who can view a variety of churches, other buildings, and the museums housed within. Even the boat ride itself, which is included in the city transportation network, is impressive, and we pass by many small, and sometimes inhabited, islands.

Our mothers leave the city by plane, and we sit once again in our house on wheels and leave by ferry. As children of nature, we enjoyed Finland a lot. The weather was terrific, with hardly any mosquitos and instead many lakes, homemade blueberry cake with hand-picked berries, and many wildlife encounters. We saw not only reindeer again, but also elk. We especially enjoyed the Finnish Lapland, and we are in agreement that we definitely want to visit again during the winter.

Above: Market display: dried meat of reindeer, elk, and deer
Below: Impressive reindeer directly on the side of the road

ELK JERKY 8€

DEER JERKY 8€

REINDEER JERKY 8€

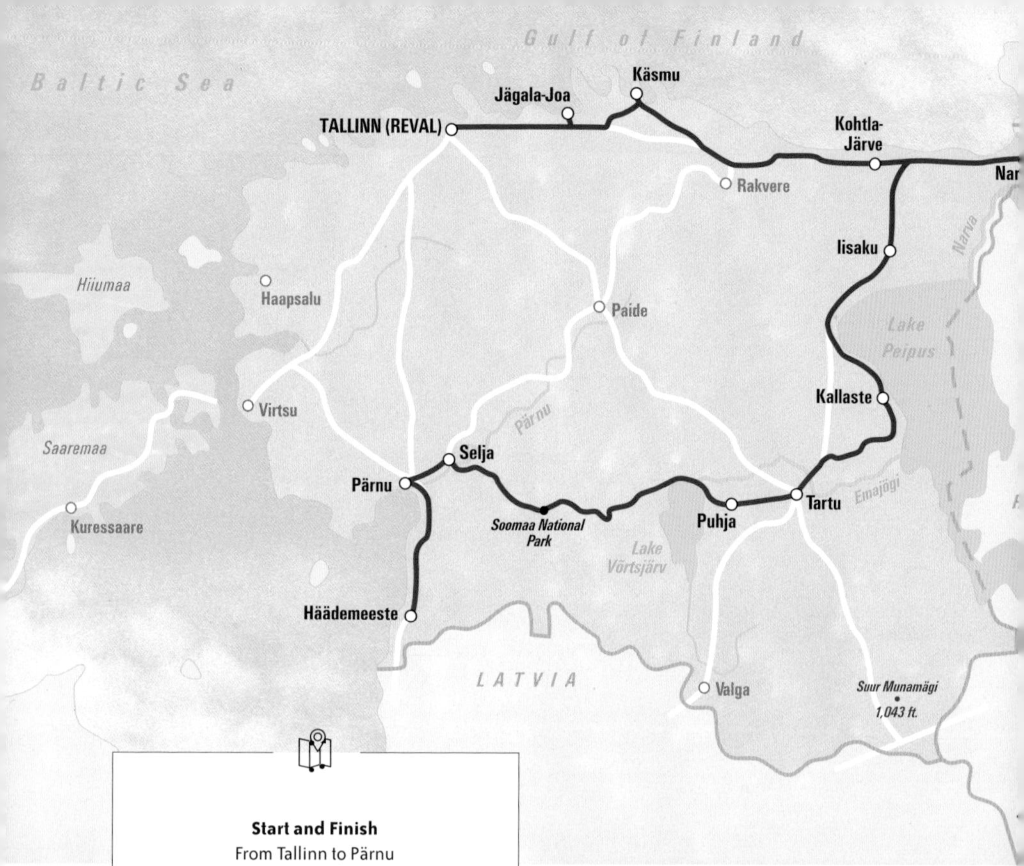

Baltic Sea

Gulf of Finland

TALLINN (REVAL)

Jägala-Joa

Käsmu

Kohtla-Järve

Nar

Rakvere

Hiiumaa

Haapsalu

Paide

Iisaku

Narva

Lake Peipus

Virtsu

Kallaste

Saaremaa

Selja

Pärnu

Pärnu

Kuressaare

Soomaa National Park

Puhja

Tartu

Emajõgi

Lake Võrtsjärv

Häädemeeste

LATVIA

Valga

Suur Munamägi
1,043 ft.

Start and Finish
From Tallinn to Pärnu

Distance
416 miles (670 km)

Travel Time
± 9 hours

Highlights
Medieval town tour of Tallinn
Hike through the Viru Bog
Narwa and Tartu
Sooma National Park

Estonia

FROM TALLINN INTO THE BOG TO NARVA AND THROUGH THE COUNTRY BACK TO THE COAST

We take the ferry directly to Tallinn, the capital city of Estonia. We park the campervan in the harbor area, where we also will spend the night. Not so pretty, but practical.

Parking lot in the harbor area
Kuunari, Tallinn (Park4Night)
59°26′34.6″ N, 24°45′23.6″ E

But the route into the city center is already beautiful—we enter the old city through a gate in the city walls. Well-kept medieval houses characterize the views: even the signs, menus, and a few shops take us back to the Middle Ages. So, a free walking tour by medieval actors fits perfectly into the scene. The cars are called funny-looking horses, the currency is—of course—"gold," and Tallinn is called Reval as it was in the old days. The ninety-minute city tour called Tales of Reval was not only entertaining but also very educational and takes place four times a day, starting at the tourist information center.

After this absolutely successful introduction, we climb to the upper city, where we can look over all of Tallin to the port and also discover the reason behind the full streets: cruise ships. But in the evening at the latest, the passengers are no longer in the city, since the food is included on the ship. We sit in the Olde Hansa restaurant, order funny-sounding dishes, and marvel at the imposingly decorated inside of the restaurant.

We stay in the city for two days, until we leave in the afternoon, headed east. Our first destination is the Jägala Waterfall.

Restaurant Olde Hansa
Vana turg 1, Tallinn
Phone: +372 627 90 20, www.oldehansa.com
Open daily from 11:00 a.m. to 11:00 p.m.,
Fridays and Saturdays until midnight
59°26′11.9″ N, 24°44′45.5″ E

Steffi swings in the forest of Käsmu

Normally, the water falls in a semicircle over the rock edge, but the hot summer of 2018 is noticeable here since the semicircle has shrunk about a quarter. The surrounding park is inviting, so we end up spending the night right here in the parking lot.

Freestanding spot at the Jägala Waterfall
Jagala-Joa tee, Koogi, 74224 Harju maakond, Estonia (Park4Night)
59°26′57.0″ N, 25°10′44.8″ E

In Lahemaa National Park, we start with a hike through the Viru Bog. We walk across wooden jetties through the impressive landscape, and from the viewing tower we can look over the whole area. It's possible to swim in a somewhat deeper bog pond, but no thanks. The privately run Camping Hiie Talu lies only a few minutes away by car. In the artist's expansive garden, we are parked next to sculptures and small frogs.

Camping Hiie Talu Kahala, Harju maakond, Harjumaa (Park4Night)
Phone: +372 56 60 70 78, peepkonton@hot.ee
Open all year
59°28′26.4″ N, 25°32′43.1″ E

Still in Lahemaa National Park, we drive along the coast of Käsmu today: a small, very pretty town. Our route along the beach leads us among the houses. Steffi is already flying high, since Lui only just found the large swing. The ground becomes increasingly sandy, and shortly after we are led through the high reeds, the large boulders from the last ice age emerge.

Following the coast farther east, we pass Altja, and since our stomachs are rumbling, Restaurant Altja sounds like just the place to go. In a small but very well-kept wooden building with fisherman's nets on the walls, traditional dishes are served. For the main course, we eat herring and have a *kama* cream for dessert. *Kama* is a powder made from different types of flour, which is mixed with quark and berries to make a very filling dessert.

A gravel road leads us to our spot for the night in the middle of the forest, and only a few steps away from the ocean. The sun shines behind the tree trunks and then disappears in the ocean.

Restaurant Altja kõrts
Altja, Lääne-Viru
Phone: +372 32 40 070, www.palmse.ee
Open daily from 12:00 p.m. to 8:00 p.m.
59°34′56.5″ N, 26°06′43.3″ E

Above: Jägala Waterfall in Lahemaa National Park
Below: Dinner at Olde Hansa in Tallinn
Following double page: Looking wistfully from Narva across the border river to Iwangorod

A beautiful spot, even if the access road wasn't the best.

**Parking lot in the forest in
Lahemaa National Park**
Mustoja, Lääne-Viru maakond (Park4Night)
59°35′04.8″ N, 26°10′29.6″ E

Along the coast we drive to the north-eastern point of Estonia and find a few nice places in Narva. The fortress with the viewing tower is beautiful, and at the university we drink something in the café and marvel at the reconstructed city hall right next to it. The newly built promenade along the Narva River is also nice.

At the transboundary Lake Peipus, we drive toward the south, along the so-called onion route. Many farming women hang their braided onion bunches out near the street. The tubers are said to give you a soft complexion. We park at the lake for the night— Russia lies on the opposite bank.

Parking lot at Lake Peipus
Kalma-Mustvee, Mustvee, Jõgeva maakond
(Park4Night)
58°50'51.7" N, 26°56'56.0" E

Tartu lies many miles away from Lake Peipus. It's a pretty university town, with many parking facilities and a nice promenade along the Emajõgi River. In the Tartu Turuhoone market hall on the river, we encounter the magic onions again, along with many other products being offered from home gardens.

The old city hides wonderful buildings— from Tartu Raekoja Plats, we look around 360 degrees and marvel at the well-kept houses.

There are even a few cafés and restaurants to be found in the main square. The restaurant that we want to go to is located at the edge of the park. Along with good dishes, the rustic ambience in the gunpowder cellar is inviting. That's also the name of the reddish beer served here: Püssirohu Punane (red gunpowder).

Restaurant Püssirohukelder
Lossi 28, Tartu
Phone: +372 730 35 55, www.pyss.ee
Open daily from 12:00 p.m. to 10:00 p.m.,
Tuesday to Saturday until 2:00 a.m.
58°22'45.9" N, 26°43'08.5" E

Then we drive all the way across Estonia from Tartu to Soomaa National Park, which is famous for its fifth season: flood season. Along the Ingatsi õpperada hike, we discover the water level markers of previous years. In some cases, the water stood up to your shoulders, and because of this, the hiking trails become canoe routes each year in the spring. The hike itself brings us to the bog, where there is a viewing tower and a bog pool for swimming, and leads us back to the starting point along another path.

After a few days, we continue driving and arrive in Pärnu, a small, cute town with a lively pedestrian area on the Rüütli street.

Of course, we look for the market hall, which ends up being located a little outside it under the name Pärnu Turg. Stocked with fresh groceries, we drive to one of the most beautiful freestanding spots, which is located just before the border to Latvia. There are already many grilling areas nicely distributed in the middle of the forest among the trees—some even with tables and benches too. There is a water source and a bathroom, which is cleaned daily and stocked with toilet paper. And yes, it is actually a freestanding spot, which is also only a few steps away from the ocean.

**Freestanding spot in the forest
(RMK Krapi Camping)**
Treimani, Pärnu (Park4Night)
57°56'22.3" N, 24°23'25.4" E

A perfect ending for our trip through Estonia. The country positively surprised us: it is modern, the yards and homes give off an almost prosperous impression, the people are friendly, and we never felt uncomfortable. The well-maintained freestanding spots and terrific nature are a welcome plus. The first Baltic country convinced us. Now we ask ourselves how the other two will be, and what the differences are. Let's go and find out—off to Latvia.

Above: Homes on Raekoja Plats in Tartu—the main square in the old city
Below: Pedestrian zone in Pärnu

30 mi.

ESTONIA

Baltic Sea

Ainaži

Valmiera

Cēsis

Gulf of Riga

Ventspils
(Windau)

Saulkrasti

Gauja

Jūrmala

Sigulda

RIGA

Dunduru Plavas

Gaising
1,024 ft.

Jelgava
(Mitau)

Venta

Aivlekste

Liepāja
(Libau)

Lielupe

Daugava (Düna)

LITHUANIA

Daugavpils
(Dünaburg)

BELAR

Start and Finish
From Gauja National Park to
Ķemeri National Park

Distance
185 miles (298 km)

Travel Time
± 4 hours, 25 minutes

Highlights
Cēsis
Wine caves in Līgatne
Bog hike
Konik horses in Ķemeri National Park

LATVIJA

70

HIKING IN NATIONAL PARKS AND ON THE SEARCH FOR NATIVE HORSES
TO THE ZEPPELIN HANGAR TO RIGA

Travel into Latvia was a piece of cake—we could simply drive in. In Sigulda, we get ourselves information about Gauja National Park in the visitor center and the drive farther to Cēsis. We make ourselves comfortable there at Camping Žagarkalns on the Gauja and light the fire in our fire pit for that evening. We like it here on the river so much that we stay a few days. The one downside: the water here at the campground smells strongly of iron, which is especially uncomfortable when showering.

Žagarkalns laivas un kempings
Mūrlejas iela 12, Cēsis, Cēsu pilsēta
(Park4Night)
Phone: +371 26 26 62 66, info@zagarkalns.lv
Open from May 15 to September 15
57°18′24.5″ N, 25°13′14.7″ E

Cēsis is a small, cute town: many flowers decorate the alleys between wooden and brick houses. In Pils Park there is an event going on for children, while the many small breweries in town, such as the Trimpus Craft Brewery, are less appropriate for them. We follow the castle wall for a while, then we go back to the campervan, which is parked next to the market hall. Of course, we visit the market as well, stock up, and keep driving. For lunch, we don't cook for ourselves today; we let that be done for us at Restaurant Vilhelmīnes dzirnavas and enjoy the beautiful weather on the terrace. After we eat, we take a walk to the Lustūzis, which are cave entrances carved into the sandstone that used to be used to store food. There are a few typical Latvian berry wines stored here—a few of which we can try, and we go ahead and take a bottle with us.

Border crossing to Latvia

Restaurant Vilhelmīnes dzirnavas
Spriņģu iela 1, Līgatne, Līgatnes pilsēta
Phone: +371 27 55 13 11
Open daily from 10:00 a.m. to 11:00 p.m.
57°14'01.3" N, 25°02'24.0" E

After a few more miles, we arrive at the spoon factory and the Vīna ražotne winery. Spoons from different kinds of wood are produced here, as well as other items, and at the same time there is a winery with sweet Latvian wines. We try some of it here too. Near Sigulda, we park our van at the end of a dead-end road in the forest and spend a quiet night there.

Freestanding spot in the forest near Sigulda
Unnamed road, Siguldas pilsēta (Park4Night)
57°09'06.4" N, 24°48'44.4" E

The next morning, we drive to Gūtmaņa ala but are a little disappointed once we arrive. Somehow, we had imagined the Gutman's Cave as something more than just a rocky cliff, even though the sandstone walls are decorated with the coats of arms of dozens of fraternities from times long past.

In Rīga, we stay true to our tradition and start our tour of the city in the market halls. The Rīgas-Centr Itirgus central market is in old airplane hangars and stretches over many streets outside. Fruits and vegetables, meat, baked goods, clothes, hardware, and flowers—the market has everything. In a few minutes, we have gone from the market into the old city, stroll through the alleys, and realize that the buildings in Rīga are built somewhat taller than in Tallinn. Rīga has its own unique character. We order the cold platter in a café and taste the regional specialties at a live concert. Afterward, we stroll slowly back to our camper.

Freestanding spot at Lake Slokas ezers
Dūņu ceļš, Jūrmala (Park4Night)
56°57'27.1" N, 23°32'47.5" E

We spend the evening in Jūrmala on the longest beach in Latvia. The sand is so compact that even bicyclists can ride on it, kids fly their kites, and some dive into the water. We decide to look for a quieter spot to spend the night on Lake Slokas ezers.

Today is a warm day, which is why we are in Ķemeri National Park early, where we go on another bog hike, which is called Lielais Ķemeru tīrelis.

Above: Gutman's Cave in Gauja National Park, with the coats of arms of student fraternities carved into the rock
Below: The old city of Rīga, with its many exciting streets

First, we go on the trail through the forest, then, using well-built jetties, we walk directly across the bog. There is a viewing tower here too, so we can view the entire bog landscape from high up.

In the exit parking lot, there is a small building with local tourist information. Steffi finds a flyer with horses on it. These Konik horses live half wild nearby, so of course we set off to find them. We drive to the Dunduru plavas fields, make our way to the viewing tower, and soon see the gray ponies with dark spinal stripes on the edge of the forest. A herd of over two hundred animals graze peacefully there, although some of them prefer to spend their time brawling. It is wonderful to be able to observe the animals in such a large herd.

As the hours pass by observing, we decide to continue to Lithuania today. We really enjoyed ourselves in Latvia—a diverse country, which is somewhat less modern than Estonia but offers good infrastructure to those traveling by camper.

Hike in Ķemeri National Park through the Lielas Ķemeru tīrelis moor

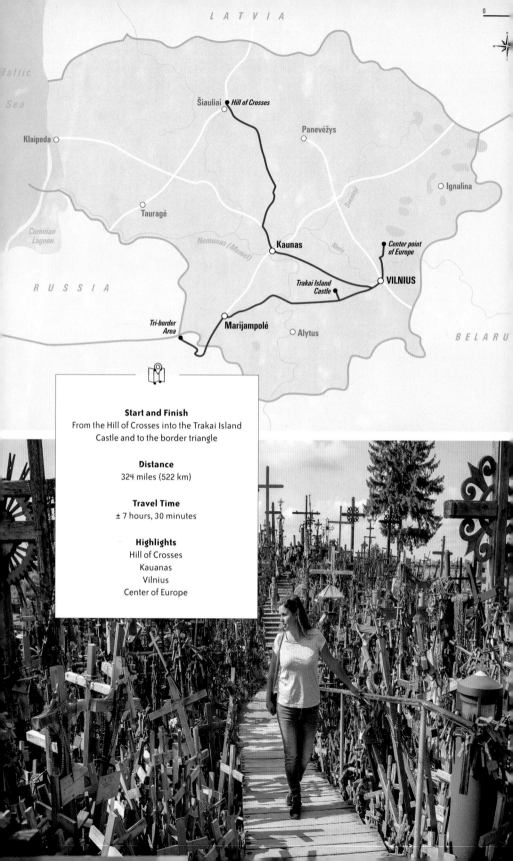

LATVIA

Baltic
Sea

Šiauliai • Hill of Crosses

Panevėžys

Klaipeda

Ignalina

Tauragė

Curonian
Lagoon

Nemunas (Memel)

Kaunas

Neris

Center point
of Europe

Šventoji

Trakai Island
Castle

VILNIUS

R U S S I A

Tri-border
Area

Marijampolė

Alytus

BELARU

Start and Finish
From the Hill of Crosses into the Trakai Island
Castle and to the border triangle

Distance
324 miles (522 km)

Travel Time
± 7 hours, 30 minutes

Highlights
Hill of Crosses
Kauanas
Vilnius
Center of Europe

Lithuania

PAST THE HILL OF CROSSES TO KAUNAS AND VILNIUS
AND TO THE BORDER TRIANGLE

In the evening, we enter our fortieth country, which is Lithuania, our last of the three Baltic countries. Just a few yards after crossing the border, we notice a few differences. Cows and goats are tied, no longer fenced, and the houses are a little more run down, even though the gardens are very well maintained. It is clearly the poorest of the three Baltic countries.

After a few miles, we reach our first destination for the night. At Sunny Nights Camping, we park under the plum trees. The campground offers many comfortable areas to just sit and chill, but Steffi is entertained in another way—a small cat catches her interest, and the two play together.

We chose this campground mostly because it's close to the Hill of Crosses. After filling up our water, which smells wonderfully like nothing but just water again, we head toward the pilgrimage site.

On-site, we see a hill, upon which stand thousands of crosses. As we approach, we also see countless small crosses, which sit among the bigger ones. We go through the narrow passages and can hardly grasp the sheer number of crosses. The legend surrounding the place is that a father at his daughter's sickbed had an apparition from an angel and was asked to put a cross on a hill. He did as he was asked, and when he arrived back home, his daughter was healed. And since many people have all different kinds of wishes, there are now an estimated 100,000 crosses on the Hill of Crosses.

Sunny Nights Camping
Rygos str. 12A, Joniškis distr., E77/A12 Road, Gataučiai
Phone: +370 626 067 35,
sunnynightscamping@gmail.com
Open from April 15 to October 15
56°09′25.3″ N, 23°32′01.8″ E

Steffi among the estimated 100,000 crosses on the Hill of Crosses

We are not religious people, but the location still left us speechless. We talk about it on our drive to Kaunas. After arriving, we park our campervan next to Kaunas Castle and stroll once around the castle grounds. A few streets farther and we're standing in front of the historic city hall, commonly known as the "white swan," which can probably be traced to the white exterior and the 174-foot (53 m) city hall tower.

Kaunas is a college town, which is something we notice immediately in the lively pedestrian zone, the many cafés, and the trendy shops. We love these types of young cities and drift through the alleys. Unfortunately, we don't get to see the beautiful avenue in the street "Laisvės alėja" because of a gigantic construction site. We would like to eat some traditional food, but it's not that easy in such a trendy city. We end up in a very nice Chinese restaurant, where it seems as if half of all the students in the city are spending their evening on the garden terrace. Full, we stroll along the banks of the Memel River back to our campervan and drive out of the city.

We found a place to spend the night at the Kaunas Reservoir, but the spot had a little too much going on during the night for our taste, so we can only partially recommend it.

After enjoying Kaunas so much, we are really looking forward to Vilnius. There is a parking lot suited for day and night where the Vilnia flows into the Neris, and this is where we park our camper and go by foot into the center of Lithuania's capital city.

Freestanding spot at the Kaunas Reservoir
Grabučiškės (Park4Night)
54°53′32.8″ N, 24°08′50.3″ E

Unfortunately, the weather is not so great, which is why we get our information about the city from the tourist information center and look at it while sitting in a café. We don't start really exploring the city until the next day. We start with a free walking tour and discover a lot about the history of the city and the many in party empty churches, which sometimes have even been converted to be used as basketball courts. We also learn from the secret passageways through the backyards that one can completely cross the city without having to go on a public street.

Freestanding spot in the center of Vilnius
T. Kosciuškos g. 1a, Vilnius (Park4Night)
54°41′16.2″ N, 25°17′38.1″ E

Above: Evening mood in the pedestrian zone of the college town of Kaunas
Below: We found a parking spot right next to Kaunas Castle.

Later, we go on our own to the Halès turgus market halls, where at the Beigelistai stand we try a traditional Jewish bagel. During the city tour, we learned that many Jews used to live here.

Vilnius is a terrific and exciting capital city. For example, there is a small, independent region within the city limits. Užupis Republika was once the poorest neighborhood, where many outlaws lived and crimes took place. Today it is a hip art district with its own hymns, president, and laws.

Back in the old city, we now also find restaurants with Lithuanian cuisine. Cold borscht soup is typical here, which arrives at our table bright pink because of the red beets inside. As a main dish, *celepelinai* are traditional here. They are filled potato dumplings in the form of a zeppelin airship. Our city tour guide recommended the restaurant Etno Dvaras, which is where we ended up.

We really enjoyed Vilnius. An exciting city with a lot of history and culture, which is not overfilled, and because of its location inland, luckily no cruise ships can dock

Restaurant Etno Dvaras
Pilies g. 16, Vilnius
Phone: +370 656 136 88, www.etnodvaras.lt
Open daily from 11:00 a.m. to midnight
54°41'0.4" N, 25°17'21.8" E

Once we finally leave the city, we don't get too far. Only 20 miles (30 km) north lies the center of Europe! Wait, this isn't the first center of Europe that we've visited. In Slovakia, we were also presented with one, and we promise you, it also won't be the last. Different ways of calculating it and unclear borders running through the Ural Mountains leave a lot of wiggle room for different results. But by just looking at the presentation, this one near Purnuškės in Lithuania is the most spectacular. We drive to Lake Galvė near Trakai, where we find a quiet parking spot for the night.

On our last day in Lithuania, we visit the Trakai Island Castle, with the name Trak salos pilis.

Freestanding spot at Lake Galvė near Trakai
Užtrakio g., Trakai (Park4Night)
54°40'11.3" N, 24°56'13.6" E

Above: Halès turgus market hall in Vilnius
Below: We explore the city center of Vilnius on a free walking tour.

Lithuania doesn't have that many well-known excursion destinations, and definitely not many that can also be reached easily by bus. Trakai, however, is one of them, and we already notice it on the basis of the parking-guidance system, the attention-grabbing souvenir stalls, the ready-to-go excursion boats, and the entrance to the castle. But it really does look beautiful. We decide on a walk around it, only to discover after arriving back at our campervan that our parking ticket, which had been expired for twenty minutes, was not safe from a parking fine. Although we still haven't ended up having to pay anything—one year later—and the ticket itself didn't look very legitimate to begin with. Let's see if something ends up coming.

Last but not least, we want to look at the border triangle of Lithuania, Poland and Russia. We always find places like this, where countries meet, exciting. We park our campervan on Polish soil and walk to the border post. We look back to Lithuania one last time and looking across to Poland, where our path is now leading us.

And so, we leave Lithuania and, with it, the Baltic countries. The third country in the group left the impression of being the poorest of the three, which is not based on its immaterial treasures. The cities were very beautiful and exciting, the food was delicious, and safety was also not a problem. Lui enjoyed Lithuania the most out of the Baltic countries, but Steffi is more neutral and found them all to be very exciting.

Above: Center of Europe at Purnuškės, at least
according to the Lithuanians
Below: Sunny Nights Camping near the Hill of Crosses

Czołpino

TouristCamp
"Czardno"

Danzig

RUSSIA

Spływy Kajakowe-
pole namiotowe
"U Małgosi"

Bachanowo

Suwałki

BELARUS

Olsztyn

Mikołajki

Narew

Białystok

Białowieża

Poznań

Vistula

Warsaw

Bug

Łódź

Gmina
Konstantynów

Lublin

Zamość

San

Katowice

Krakau

0   50 mi.

Start and Finish
From the coast, through Gdansk, and the Masurian Lakes to Krakow

Distance
874 miles (1406 km)

Travel Time
Approximately 20 hours

Highlights
Sand Dunes and Gdansk
Masuria and Wilderness
Zamosc and Krakow

Poland

FROM THE COAST TROUGH MASURIA
TO THE PRIMEVAL FOREST

Our exploration tour of Poland begins at the Baltic Sea in the northernmost part of the country. What awaits us isn't just an endless beach but immense sand dunes. This region belongs to the Słowiński National Park, and the most famous dune landscape is located around Łeba. Since it's still the last week of summer vacation, we opt for a smaller dune near Czołpino, hoping it's less crowded. It's also within the national park, so we have to pay both the parking fee for our camper and the national park entrance fee. We set off on foot through the vast pine forest, passing by the lighthouse, down to the beach. Ahead of us is the Baltic Sea, an endless beach to the right and left, and very few other visitors. We choose to go right and stroll along the beach for over an hour. Unfortunately, we don't find any amber. Not far away, we settle in for the night at the SurferCamp by Lake Gardno.

After so much beautiful nature, we crave a city. On our way to Gdansk, we pass through the Kashubian Switzerland, a natural park with many hills and lakes; hence the "Switzerland" in its name. The former Hanseatic city of Gdansk is large, industrial, but its Old Town is easily explored on foot. We find a well-located and free parking spot near the Old Town and are in the center within minutes. The buildings are stunning to look at, especially Long Market Street with its grand buildings. Just around the corner is St. Mary's Church, whose tower you can even climb. And of course, the Hala Targowa market halls are a must-see. Gdansk is also known for amber. This is evident from the many small shops selling jewelry and other amber items to passing tourists. Steffi stays strong since she already bought a lovely amber bracelet in Lithuania. After an exciting day in Gdansk, we decide to spend the night right in the parking lot by the small marina. A parking spot for a city couldn't be more perfect.

SurferCamp Gardno
Gardno, 76-213 Retowo, Poland
Phone: +48 601 655 189
www.surfcamp-gardno.com
Open from May 1 to September 30
54°38 02.2 N, 17°08 20.9 E

Free Parking Spot Gdansk
Tramwaj wodny—F6, 80-752 Gdańsk, Poland
54°21 13.1 N, 18°3955.8 E

Above: Mushroom yield after our hike in Masuria
Below: Masuria is known for its water sport opportunities.

We've heard a lot about the Masurian Lakes in Poland, so we decide to visit the region. On the way, we pass through Malbork and visit the world's largest Gothic castle—impressive! In Mikołajki, the tourist center of Masuria, we settle down at Camping Wagabunda and explore the town on foot along Lake S´niardwy, the largest of the Masurian Lakes.

Camping Wagabunda
Ul. Leśna 2, Mikołajki
Phone: +48 87 421 60 18
wagabunda-mikolajki@wagabunda-mikolajki.pl
Open from May 1 to September 30
53°47 43.6 N, 21°33 54.0 E

The best and most popular starting point for canoe trips in Masuria is Krutyn´. At the Krutynia River, we launch our boat, and now we have a choice from up to 62 miles (100 kilometers) of routes. We go for a hike to the nearby three lakes, located in a large moor. Along the way, we find some chanterelles and even a big cep mushroom (warning: do not pick or eat mushrooms without professional oversight). Mushroom risotto takes too long for lunch, so we go to the Mazurska restaurant across from the parking lot. Lui chooses fresh fish, while Steffi goes for her Polish favorite, pierogi.

Restauracja Mazurska
Krutyn´, 34a
Phone: +48 89 742 14 40
www.mazurska.pl
53°41 11.2 N, 21°25 47.1 E

Now we want to explore Masuria off the beaten path. For that, we drive to Połom, where we park our van in the meadow of Adventure Camp U Małgosi. Here, we have not only a fire pit with seating but also a private pier into the river—cool! The next morning, the owner's son arrives with his car and a kayak in tow. We sit in a tandem kayak on a sandbank; he gives us a push into the water and says, "Have fun!" Uh, which way do we even go? Well, just follow the river. We do that for the next three hours. The narrow river meanders beautifully through the forest and passes through closely spaced reed seas, and by pretty sandbanks with barbecue areas. With quite heavy arms from paddling, we finally spot our small wooden pier, and behind it, our campervan. We're back at camp! What a fantastic kayaking tour.

Adventure Camp + Kayak Rental U Małgosi
At the Łaźna Struga River, Połom 2/2, 19-411, Poland
Phone: +48 791 148 355
splywyumalgosi@gmail.com
53°58 43.6 N, 22°16 19.6 E

Last, we turn our attention to the Suwałki Region. Lake Hańcza is the deepest lake in Poland, attracting deepwater divers with its clear waters. Today, it's too chilly for swimming, but we're here for a different reason. Not far away, a Swiss couple has been making cheese according to Swiss recipes for over thirty years, and what's special about them is that they make Swiss cheese in the farthest corner of Poland. We search in vain for a sign that says "Cheese Factory" or something similar.

Above: A nice bicycle route goes around Lake Wigry.
Below: A beautiful monastery next to Lake Wigry

But we have the coordinates, and we find the remote farm. As soon as we park, the owners come around the corner, delighted to welcome Swiss visitors. Even after thirty years in Poland, both of them still speak perfect Swiss German. They tell us their story while chicks flutter around us. Finally, we get to taste the cheese. Mmmm, it's delicious! Of course, we buy some before bidding farewell and heading to Camping Widok in the Wigry National Park.

Swiss Cheese Farm
Bachanowo 21, 16-404 Jeleniewo, Poland
Phone: +48 87 568 35 35
www.realearth.pl
54°13 52.8 N, 22°48 23.8 E

What a breathtaking view! The campground is situated on several tiers, and from each one you can enjoy a fantastic view of Lake Wigry. Its shore is dotted with peninsulas and reed forests. A flat meadow lines the shore at the campsite, from where piers lead into the lake, where kayaks and paddleboats await renters. We don't even bother connecting our campervan to the power grid before slipping into our bathing suits and jumping into the lake. The water is wonderfully clear and has the perfect temperature. Later, we have a picnic for dinner, of course with the delicious Swiss cheese. We actually stay at the campground

for two nights. The next day, we grab two bicycles and cycle around Lake Wigry. A great bike path covers 28 miles (45 kilometers) around the lake, passing through forests, over wooden boardwalks, past beautiful swimming spots, and by the gorgeous Wigry Monastery. In the evening, we enjoy dinner at the restaurant connected to the campground.

Camping Widok
Bryzgiel 7, 16-304, Poland
Phone: +48 502 304 588
www.bryzgiel.pl
53°59 59.5 N, 23°04 57.6 E

As we prepare our campervan for the next leg of our journey, we look forward to our next special destination. Europe also has a primeval forest! A primeval forest is defined as never having been touched by human hands—no logging, no cultivation, and no planting. Since 1932, this cross-border forest in Poland has been a national park, with the core zone accessible only with park rangers on guided tours, due to its high protection status. Here, the last wild European bison roam.

At the national park office in Białowieza, we learn about the national park and the possibilities it offers. Right next door, we can rent bicycles for seven euros per day. Since it's already early evening, we postpone our exploration until tomorrow.

Above: The colorful building exteriors of Zamość are strongly reminiscent of Italy.
Below: Buying Swiss Cheese in Poland—a welcome experience

PTTK Białowieza
Guide Service in the National Park
Kolejowa 17, Białowieza
Phone: +48 85 681 22 95
www.pttk.bialowieza.pl
52°42 00.8 N, 23°50 39.1 E

We spend the night in the parking lot of the Białowieza Wildlife Park, a peaceful spot except for the sounds of animals. Occasionally, wolves or bison may howl.

Free Camping Spot Rezerwat Pokazowy Zubrow
Białowieza (Park4Night)
52°42 15.9 N, 23°47 42.7 E

In the morning, we park behind the national park office, pick up our bikes, and start cycling. We choose a route that doesn't enter the core zone but still passes through the national park, and we can explore this area on our own. We pass by the old Białowieza train station, ride through Pałakowy Park with its charming buildings and ponds, see the locomotive of the narrow-gauge railway, and eventually reach Lake Topiło. Here, we turn around after a picnic break and take a different route back. By the end of the day, we've covered about 31 miles (50 kilometers) on our bicycles.

Tired from the day, we sleep again at the wildlife park. Only the next morning do we continue southward and take two rest days by the Bug River, which marks the border with Belarus here.

Free Camping Spot by the Bug River
Gmina Konstantynow (Park4Night)
52°16 44.9 N, 23°09 24.4 E

Only after this break do we head to Zamosc, a Polish city with an Italian flair. A Venetian architect contributed to the city's appearance, and the colorful houses on the Rynek Wielki main square indeed make it seem like Venice without canals. The old town center is quite manageable, and we have a small meal before moving on.

Krakau, better known as Krakow, is a popular tourist destination, as we immediately notice on-site. It feels like hundreds of golf carts have been transformed into tourist vehicles, chattering in various languages as they navigate the old town alleys. The city, however, is beautiful. We stroll through the streets, pass by the Krakow Cloth Hall—the market hall—and, of course, walk through the beautiful building itself. Here on the main square is also St. Mary's Church and numerous restaurants. Slightly south is Wawel Castle, perched on a hill. It's a whole complex, including a church and a palace. It's surrounded by a castle wall and, farther on, a park, where there's even a fire-breathing dragon. We follow the Vistula River to the Jewish Quarter, where we find many trendy street food stalls and restaurants. In the restaurant Hamsa, we let ourselves be enchanted by Israeli cuisine right in the heart of Poland.

Above: An endless beach along the coast of the Baltic Sea
Below: View over the market hall to St. Mary's Basilica in Kraków

Restaurant Hamsa
Szeroka 2, Krakow
Phone: +48 515 15 01 45
www.hamsa.pl
Open daily from 10 a.m. to 11 p.m., Saturday
and Sunday from 9 a.m.
50°03 11.3 N, 19°56 51.6 E

In the twilight, we take a stroll through the center, then take a taxi back to Kemping Clepardia, where our campervan is waiting for us.

Kemping Clepardia
Henryka Pachon´skiego 28, Krakow (Par-
k4Night)
Phone: +48 12 415 96 72
clepardia@gmail.com
Open from April 15 to October
15 50°05 43.0 N, 19°56 28.8 E

And so ends our journey through Poland. It's a vast country where you could travel for years and still not see everything. We discovered fascinating corners and enjoyed excellent food. Additionally, Poland remains one of the most affordable countries in Europe for us.

Our lovely view on the Camping Widok

Start and Finish
From Valletta to the neighboring island of Gozo

Distance
88 miles (142 km)

Travel Time
± 5 hours, 35 minutes

Highlights
Valletta
Marsaxlokk
Mdina
Gozo

Malta

WINTER ISLAND
EXPLORATION

Malta will never lie on our route but of course belongs to the forty-seven European countries. We take the ferry to the southern part of the small country and could already marvel at Valletta's beauty from the water. Traffic drives on the left again, but after our experiences in Great Britain and Ireland, it takes Steffi only 200 yards to be back in her element.

We park our campervan on Manoel Island and take the passenger ferry into the center. The whole fortress city counts as a UNESCO World Heritage Site. No wonder—we immediately feel like we have stepped back in time.

Out and about in the city center, we continually marvel at the terrific buildings, almost all of which are composed of colorfully painted wood. We stroll through the streets and pass the Upper Barrakka Gardens, where we enjoy the terrific view of the harbor. We stroll back slowly, because even though our parking spot was recommended as a possible place to spend the night, we would rather

drive a little farther away from all the hustle and bustle. We find a quiet spot in Rinella Bay with a view of Valletta and stay. Unfortunately, the night doesn't pass as quietly as we expected—a few teenagers test the sound systems in their cars until about two in the morning . . .

Freestanding spot in Rinella Bay
Rinella, Il-Kalkara
35°53'35.0"N 14°31'34.7"E

Marsaxlokk is the next spot on our itinerary. It's a small fishing village with a boardwalk worth visiting. There are many colorful wooden boats anchored in the clear water. There is a market taking place along the boardwalk, and on Sundays fish is also sold there. On the way back, we see the Pastizzeria Sphinx, and in their display case we discover the Maltese specialty, *pastizzi*. We try all three kinds of the strudel pastry, filled with cheese, pea mousse, and chicken.

Top left: The colorful fishing boats in Marsaxlokk Harbor
Top right: The traditional Maltese food—*pastizzi*
Below: The typical bay windows in Valletta

We drink a cold *cisk* with it: a local Maltese beer.

The St. Peter pools are only a few minutes away from the town. The ocean shows a true splendor of colors here and a place to comfortably go swimming or, like so many, bravely jump from the cliffs into the water.

Tonight, we park at the Dingli Cliffs, enjoy a wonderful sunset, and have a comfortably quiet night here in the middle of nowhere.

A rainy day allows us to drive a little more efficiently than planned, which is why we already reach Gozo the next day and are ultimately so happy about this turn of events. We would have never dedicated so much time to the small island.

Dingli Cliffs freestanding spot
Between Dingli and Si iewi
35°50′42.6″ N, 14°23′48.2″ E

We cross the short distance by ferry and drive to the main town of Victoria, another beautiful medieval city, known for its citadel with its fortification walls. We take a look after eating a Maltese cold platter in the Piazza Café in front of the St. George's Basilica.

In the afternoon, we drive to the Azure Window, even though this stone arch was destroyed by a powerful storm. This part of the coast is beautiful anyway, and above all we find a place to spend the night that would make the heart of any freestanding camper soar. Parked on the cliffs, we look out at the water and fall asleep to the sounds of the ocean.

Azure Window freestanding spot
Triq Il Gebla Tal General, San Lawrenz
36°02′59.4″ N, 14°11′27.6″ E

Yesterday, we saw a terrific church along our route, which is why we drive to the Ta' Pinu Basilica and take a closer look. An impressive building. After viewing it, we continue along the street, which gets increasingly narrow, and arrive at Wied il-Mielaħ. There is apparently another stone arch in Malta, but it is not reachable by travel bus. We think that's good and enjoy the moment here for ourselves. Originally, we already wanted to go back to the mainland today, but a few hundred yards farther we find a spot where we must stay. A freestanding spot on the cliff with a view of the ocean, far from any civilization. We meet up with friends who happen to be in the area.

Above: The Ta' Pinu Basilica piqued our interest when we drove by.
Below: Our spot for the night at the Azure Window on the island of Gozo

For two nights, the four of us enjoy this perfect spot just to ourselves. The stone shaft somewhat east of our freestanding spot is also worth seeing—we were there at sunset. We visit Wied il-Għasri farther on; it is a cove similar to a fjord that pushes itself inland and is pretty to look at. Next are the salt plains farther along the narrow coastal road. There are countless pools carved into the stone—the salt comes from the sea water in the summer. In the small coastal town of Marsalforn, we buy ourselves some more *pastizzi*, which is our snack for the ferry that will now bring us back to the main island of Malta.

Popeye Village is located very close to the ferry harbor, which was used for the backdrop of the 1979 *Popeye* film. We go past the entrance on foot, follow the street a little, and now have the perfect view of the re-created fishing village.

Freestanding spot at the cliffs of Wied il-Għasri
Gravel road between Wied il-Mielaħ and Wied il-Għasri
36°04'48.3" N, 14°13'0.8" E

Fantastic pitch on the cliffs near Wied il-Mielaħ

We let the evening come to an end in Sea View Café in Il-Mellieħa. From there, we look over the whole Mellieħa Bay. We spend the night in Mellieħa itself on the only more-or-less-official parking lot in all of Malta. Additionally, it's the only place where one is able to dispose of gray and black water (gray is the water from the dishwasher, black water is from the toilet) behind the public toilets and fill up with fresh water (connection in the men's toilets).

Our ferry already leaves tonight for Sicily, so we want to use the day to look at the old capital city of Mdina. Already upon entering the gates to the city, we feel as if time has stood still here. The medieval city is in perfect shape, and the typical sandstone for Malta makes the buildings built with it shine in the sunlight. The streets are narrow, but wide enough for the small carriages to pass, which was more important in the past than it is today. We totally lose ourselves in the flair of Medina and in the countless small details such as the unique streetlights or the interesting, small shops.

Parking spot at Area Sosta Camper Mellieħa
Għadira, Mellieħa
35°58′27.7″ N, 14°20′59.6″ E

Since Malta is not too complicated and the distances are short, we are back at the ferry harbor in Valletta in no time. The time has come to try the national drink there. *Kinnie* is a carbonated soft drink made from bitter oranges and herbal extracts and tastes delicious ice cold. And then, we must already board the fastest ferry in Europe. In an hour and a half, we will already be back on Sicily.

We really enjoyed Malta and especially Gozo, and even though there is only minimal infrastructure for campers, it is one of the countries with the most-beautiful spots to spend the night. It's a shame that it's so far away, but that's probably for the best so the small island remains the undiscovered jewel that it is.

Above: Interesting decorations in the streets of Victoria on Gozo
Below: In the capital city of Malta—Mdina

Recollections

UKRAINE
OUR TRAVEL DIARY FROM THE YEAR 2018

Unfortunately, even in today's world, new wars are ignited, even in Europe. Thus, in 2018, during our grand European journey, we were able to visit three more countries that one should not travel to today due to the precarious security situation. However, we'd like to tell you about our weeklong road trip through Ukraine. The people, cities, and landscapes we had the privilege to experience were far too remarkable for us not to share at least some of it with you.

Coming from Poland, we entered Ukraine in September 2018. At the Ukrainian border, we embarked on a small marathon—obtaining all the necessary stamps and paying a fee. The officers were friendly and helpful; one of them even sang a bit.

As we traveled through the country, we noticed some unfamiliar car brands, and all the shops had signs in Cyrillic script. Thankfully, the road signs were also in Latin letters. We felt a significant cultural difference from Poland, and the traffic was very uncoordinated, especially when we entered Lviv. It required a lot of patience, but we learned that being assertive was the key.

In Lviv, we visited several parking lots as potential places to spend the night. One was in the middle of an intersection, another in a dark backyard that didn't seem suitable for sleeping. We couldn't find anything suitable, so we ended up staying in a hotel, where we could securely park our campervan in a locked backyard. That same evening, we walked to the city center, found ourselves in the lively old town, listened to street musicians, had a beer at a three-story beer theater while a jazz band performed live, and felt completely safe even on the way back.

The next morning, we extended our hotel stay and began the day with a free walking tour. The incredibly likable city guide explained the city's history, took us through beautiful streets, and led us to a secret underground bar that required a password for entry. We found Lviv to be really cool! Many restaurants and bars invited us to linger for a long time on the second evening. We followed our city guide Anastacia's restaurant recommendation and ended up at the Ribs Restaurant "At Arsenal." When there was a table available, we were led to the basement, past two large rotating grills with dozens of racks of ribs.

The menu was small, but those who came here wanted to eat ribs, and so did we. There was no cutlery, but plenty of household paper towels. A unique atmosphere and the world's best ribs. We wondered what this city was doing to us, because we were blown away by the atmosphere of Lviv!

We would love to stay in such places forever, but we continued our journey. What else lay ahead? Outside the city, the houses quickly became small and old, with prosperity concentrated in the urban areas. The roads varied from very new and good to completely destroyed, with many potholes and ruts up to 7.8 inches (20 centimeters) deep in the asphalt. We drove through Ivano-Frankivsk and into the western Carpathians. We passed a waterfall, where we also stopped. Steffi strolled through the souvenir market and played with a stray puppy, while Lui, mean-while, critically observed the perfectly posed stone eagles, ready for a photo.

In fact, here in the Carpathians, we found a campground, or something like it. We parked behind Misha's house on a meadow in the evening. The owner spoke Ukrainian, Russian, six words of German, and four of English. He made a fire under the water boiler, and later we could take a warm shower. Lui felt sympathy for the man, who lived alone there. So he grabbed our bottle of Swiss quince schnapps and offered him a schnapps. The owner was very pleased, and the schnapps was quickly shared. He disappeared into the building, only to return shortly afterward with his own bottle of clear spirits.

How this evening ended can probably be imagined by everyone. There were definitely no more language barriers, and the next day, Steffi took the wheel. Our journey continued through the western Carpathians.

We traveled to the southernmost part of the country, to the border river with Romania. We were tempted to simply cross the border back into Romania, but we also wanted to see more of Ukraine. Now came a highlight for us as European travelers: the center of Europe! For those who have read the previous chapters—especially Slovakia and Lithuania—you know we had already been to two other self-proclaimed centers of Europe and can only laugh about it now. But this one received a special award: it was the only one with a restaurant right next to it and was henceforth considered the tastiest center in all of Europe. The restaurant was a sight in itself due to its interior decoration. There was even a single English menu, but the waitress had a hard time figuring out how to say the dish's name in Ukrainian.

The food we received was incredibly delicious. We continued along the Romanian border for a long time. The road was some-times in very poor condition, with deep ruts and large potholes. We could drive at only about 31 miles (50 km) per hour, making for very slow progress. We made a stop at Palanok Castle, which could be visited.

Just outside the city, we found a camp-ground by a small lake. It was intended more for tents than for campervans, but our compact campervan fit into one of the plots, and we spent our last night in Ukraine by the lake.

The contrasts in Ukraine were significant, whether in terms of buildings, vehicles, or road conditions. However, the people were incredibly friendly, and many spoke English, especially in urban areas. We noticed that many people always had a smile on their faces. This positive atmosphere contributed to our extreme comfort in the country. And Lviv was in a league of its own, the most fascinating city we had visited in Europe so far.

And even as we left the country heading towards Slovakia, we promised ourselves that we would come back to see more of Ukraine. Whether we can keep that promise to ourselves is now uncertain, and it pains us to know what these positive and hospitable people have been going through since the beginning of the war in February 2022.

AND HERE WE WOULD LIKE TO SHOW YOU A FEW PICTURES OF OUR EXCITING TIME IN UKRAINE.

45 out of *47 Countries* – what happens *Next*

ICELAND AND KAZAKHSTAN STILL WAIT FOR US

That was thirty-seven tours through forty-two European countries and memories of our journey through Ukraine. For those who have been keeping count, we have currently traveled to forty-five countries in Europe, so two are still missing. One of them is Iceland. The island in the north was originally on the plan for the summer of 2019, but other projects came up, and we want to dedicate at least three weeks to exploring Iceland. Steffi would like even more time, since she is particularly fond of Icelandic horses and would like to go on a multiday riding tour.

And the other missing country is Kazakhstan. But you might be thinking, Kazakhstan isn't in Europe. However, we are orienting ourselves on the basis of geographical Europe, which includes the part of Kazakhstan west of the Ural Mountains.

In fact, Russia and Turkey also span two continents and are counted among our forty-seven countries. And since we're on the topic of border cases, we're not including Cyprus and Georgia, since geographically they do not belong to the continent of Europe.

But for this book, our journey temporarily ends here, though in reality, it's far from over. We've also filmed our entire tour and uploaded it to YouTube. In over three hundred videos, we take you along with us through Europe. So if you haven't had enough, you can simply check out "comewithus2" on YouTube.

We wish you safe travels and always at least a hand's breadth of space around your campervan!

Warm regards from your fellow travelers,

Steffi Rickenbacher and Lui Eigenmann

Above: Railway hike on Pelion in Greece
Below: One of the best pass roads in Norway: Snøvegen

INDEX

Published by Schiffer Publishing, Ltd.
4880 Lower Valley Road
Atglen, PA 19310
Phone: (610) 593-1777; Fax: (610) 593-2002
Email: info@schifferbooks.com
Web: www.schifferbooks.com

For our complete selection of fine books on this and related subjects, please visit our website at www.schifferbooks.com. You may also write for a free catalog.

Schiffer Publishing's titles are available at special discounts for bulk purchases for sales promotions or premiums. Special editions, including personalized covers, corporate imprints, and excerpts, can be created in large quantities for special needs. For more information, contact the publisher.